FLOW

Published in 2017
by Flow Academy

ISBN 978-1-5272-0985-5

Design concept and cover design: Evelin Kasikov
Graphic design and illustration: Anna Jarvis
Editor: Jennifer Marston

Printed by Park Communications Limited,
London E6 6LA

FIN GOULDING
HAYDN SHAUGHNESSY

A Handbook for Change-Makers, Mavericks, Innovation Activists and Leaders

SIMPLIFYING DIGITAL TRANSFORMATION

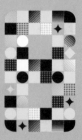

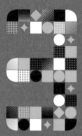
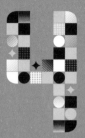

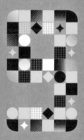

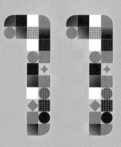

INTRODUCTION

CREATING A CULTURE CHANGE AT WORK IS ONE OF THE BIG UNSOLVED MYSTERIES OF MODERN BUSINESS.

It's a strange Agatha Christie-like mystery with no ending and a long line of corpses in the drawing room: the people who tried culture change all the way up to digital transformation and failed.

The right culture creates extraordinary adaptability and is your ticket to a more productive organisation. It is gold dust, titanium-tipped pens and diamond-studded spectacles all in one. Every enterprise wants it but what exactly is this thing we call good culture?

It is partly the ability to think like a startup, which involves a set of attributes we will define later. And it is partly the ability to work within a digital environment, which has created an entirely new context for business.

Think of it in three ways:

1 **Scale** A digital, adaptive company will use very advanced IT, which allows it to scale new business quickly to an unprecedented size.

2 **Scope** This company will likely be ambitious in the range of customers it serves. It will have changed the way it views the role of the firm, developing a wider diversity of products and services to meet more needs.

3 **Speed** It will have systems in place for continuous decision-making, which means it will be operating with a new kind of "velocity" or speed, as business becomes more real-time.

In order to achieve scale, scope, and speed, companies need a new type of engagement from staff. That's the holy grail and the reason why culture change is so significant.

Before we can approach this new culture, though, we have to ask: Why don't people, ordinarily, enjoy work enough to invest more of their ingenuity, creativity, passion, and guile into it?

This book provides you with the answers to that question as well as the perfect model for how to create great culture using a new set of visualisation tools and social principles.

Culture change is a serious business

The reason people don't offer up their ingenuity at work is that the rules we work by often bring us into conflict with each other and the values of the firm. From an employee standpoint, people find themselves or their ideas rejected by the organisation in ways that cause them distress. Or they witness their colleagues experience something similar.

Rejection can come through a bad boss ridiculing an employee in response to an idea (sending the clear message to everyone else: "Get back, close up, don't take chances"). Or people are railroaded into "alignment", a catch-all cultural rule for not stepping out of line. Or rejection can happen when people feel they must endure interminable meetings that don't allow them a real voice. In those meetings, they witness their bosses making glaring errors of judgment and, instead of speaking up, they do what they think the company most wants of them. They stay "aligned".

Paradoxically, at the same time these people are urged to speak up, take risks and be creative!

What you see in these situations, and they are pervasive, is a failure of management to lead change, dressed up as a failure of motivation and commitment on the part of employees.

These conditions force people to retreat into their personal silos. The sense of isolation that stems from this is further exacerbated by HR policies that emphasise individual achievement. In an era when maximum collaboration is needed, our leadership practices are creating silos of one.

We have the ability to replace these contradictory emotional currents. We can work to a pleasing melody rather than a drumbeat

For **flow** masters, people who broadly follow the principles of this book, culture reflects the quality of human interactions in the workplace. Instead of the tensions that accompany traditional hierarchy we can focus instead on making good social interaction a mechanism for increasing the value that we create together. We can liberate ourselves from the past, though, of course, we must do this within guide rails

that respect one overriding principle: the need to create additional value for customers.

Like it or not, the essence of working in our new digital environment is that people have to do more within constrained resources. The new economy makes extraordinary demands on us, which carries more potential for unspoken conflict.

Ironically, the language of innovation is often what gets in the way.

Most studies of innovation, hence most of the knowledge of how we adapt the workplace to changing market requirements, have focused on the process for developing new products and services.

Innovation studies often purport to describe a common formula for innovation (the seven steps to corporate heaven or the five stages to a more creative you). In reality, innovation studies are likely to be reporting on exceptional cases that caught a writer or academic's attention. That gives us case studies based on special circumstances and unusually talented or insightful people. It does not give us evidence or examples of how to change work processes, which is the essence of digital transformation.

Problems aside, many people enjoy the challenge of delivering solutions and value propositions across more products and services, at greater scale and higher velocity. This is good culture.

What digital transformation needs more than anything is better processes to create scale, scope, and speed.

We know, but often ignore, the fact that good product or service innovation forces companies to change a process somewhere in their organisation—all change comes back to process. But we do very little learning about what we, Fin and Haydn, call **process-model innovation.**

In today's high-performing organisations, product and process have become one and the same. New ways of constructing IT architecture (DevOps and microservices especially, but don't let's get bogged down in technical terms) radically alter what is possible in the way we serve customers.

We ignore that process reality and instead continue to talk about business-model innovation, open innovation, or design thinking. However, the result of all these techniques will, more and more, be connected to a new process.

That means today's innovators change how we get things done, not just what we produce.

Process-model innovation, inevitably, also changes how we interact with each other. Change in marketing, technology, data, etc., implicitly means a change to the way people work together and in the structure and language of their interactions. They have more data to hand, more knowledge of customers, new techniques and more opportunities to create value.

Today, this panoply of synchronised change is extremely important because most good organisations need to be innovating their products, services, and processes in harmony, and do it multiple times **per day.**

Really?
Yes.

Travel site SkyScanner aims to update its many services thousands of times a day! That's velocity and scale for you and it will become the norm.[1]

Why?

Software infrastructure enables change of this magnitude, and data provides the feedback loops that suggest what should happen next. Meanwhile, customers constantly demand more. These factors working together create the need for companies to innovate on a daily basis.

So, when people reference a **culture of innovation—** or **thinking like a startup**—they're actually talking about our capacity to create and manage changes in the way things get done. In digital transformation, we aim to effect these changes at scale, scope, and speed.

[1]

Read all about it here:

http://codevoyagers.com/2016/11/07/from-20-to-2-million-releases-a-year-part-3/

Puppet.com's Annual State of Devops gives evidence of the goodness:

https://puppet.com/sites/default/files/inline-images/2016%20State%20of%20DevOps%20infographic.jpg

We, Fin and Haydn, believe that processes mirror the culture surrounding them. In fact, culture can't be anything else than process and interaction melded together to create value.

In **flow**, the philosophy this book outlines, process is social interaction. All good change comes back to the quality of interaction between people. Work "structure" becomes the shaping of social interaction by leaders who enable people to co-create process "on the fly".

If people interact well, they can co-create processes that liberate a company from silos and bad rules. By making decisions in the flow, they can make the firm vastly more innovative and productive. Would you trust employees this far? If you hesitate, then you are part of the problem. You are seeking rules and guarantees that no longer have validity.

Flow is emerging naturally around us in great companies that have truly unlocked employee creativity (as opposed to those who mandate it).

In today's economy, process-model innovation eats all other forms of culture for lunch. A good culture makes processes adaptive, effective, and value driven. But for good culture to happen, you first need to clean out the inappropriate and stifling processes that have so far dominated most workplaces.

There are zombie processes—the bad ones that won't go away— everywhere in companies today, built on outdated rules that people in the change game still have to comply with. They inhibit good work and prevent the kind of learning environment that allows a culture of innovation to grow.

Nobody, of course, wants to be a disciple of bad process. But here is some startling evidence: researchers who have studied different types of innovation find that:[2]

Most firms are more likely to create and maintain skillsets around innovating new products rather than innovating the way things get done. They emphasise **skills in product development,** not **process innovation.**

Even firms that do innovate well over time do not maintain **persistent process innovation.**

Firms that fail in these respects do so because **they fail to build a way to learn from experience.**

Without addressing these issues (build, change, learn), you cannot cost-effectively improve the way you serve your customers. Nor can you keep up with companies already cracking the code on this vital competitive advantage.

In **flow**, bad processes are stalked down and overrun, and good culture triumphs. The result is continuous innovation, success, value, goodness, and Corporate Gold.

The chief method we use in **flow** is visualisation. By bringing more into the open in a company, we can stimulate more interaction and support people in uncovering more value.

[2]

David Córcoles, Ángela Triguero, and María Carmen Cuerva (2016). Comparing Persistence of Product and Process Innovation: A Discrete-Time Duration Analysis of Innovation Spells.

Economics: The Open-Access, Open-Assessment E-Journal, 10 (2016-32): 1—35.

http://dx.doi. org/10.5018/economics-ejournal.ja.2016-32

At one client site where we recently worked, software that lay unused and unloved actually had a market value of $4 billion (measured by the fact that a startup using this type of software had realised a $4 billion IPO).

By visualising the company's assets, we were able to set the software in front of executives to exploit as they might wish. It was one of several assets being underutilised. But now executives can see this. It has been visualised on a wall rather than being buried in a server.

Most organisations have these overlooked assets or assets that can readily be brought to market if only they can gain visibility rather than being hidden away under all the waste that organisations typically generate.

The news for conventional management is that the processes that manifest this value rely on people not technology. Which is another way of saying good process is not something you can buy from a vendor. It relies on different moods, emotions, relationships, personal dynamics, interpersonal dependencies, laughter, competitiveness, and ambition. Ugly or exhilarating or both.

Flow is a different way of working. Complementing Agile and Lean processes, it is a set of principles for managing continuous change but with a very special twist: in **flow**, people co-create the work**flow** and co-decide the best way to create more value.

So this is not a book about strategy, though the theory matters very much to how your strategy evolves. With **flow**, you can push aside many common barriers to growth, update to the digital future, and achieve more. Your strategy will become more ambitious and diversified, and less costly. **Flow** culture can make you bigger and stronger if that's what your heart cries out for. But if not, it can simply make work better for employees, more productive for the firm, and enhance your capacity to create value in whatever market you choose.

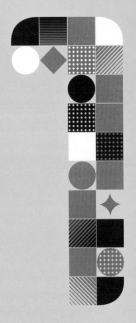

WE ALL WANT CHANGE

HAYDN ONCE WALKED INTO A SHOP AND ASKED FOR A PARTICULAR TYPE OF PEN.

"None left," the store owner said.
"People keep buying them."
Goddamn those customers!

That attitude, that somehow the stakeholder is to blame for a businesses' shortcomings, is exactly how the workplace functions today.

Rather than the customer being blamed, however, it is the employee. Companies big and small are full of managers who intuitively reject the notion that they should change then blame the lack of it on resistance from staff. Or they force a change-management project, in effect a new set of rules, onto a situation where more freedom to create—the freedom you get with **flow**—would be a more rational course of action.

Yet there are few things people want more than to work differently and creatively and to learn something new each day.

Is it possible to learn something new every day?

In traditional work environments, the answer would be an emphatic "No!"

Continuous learning, though, is one of those evangelical phrases espoused by leaders. We all need to learn more each day. Learning is the essence of being able to function differently. As a society, and as enterprises, however, we often lack the tools, or sometimes the will, to embed the concept of continuous learning (or continuous improvement) into how we work.

The workforce asked to commit itself to continuous learning is the one that is constantly given easily mastered tasks that become repetitive and undemanding all too quickly.

Leaders want people to sit tucked away in neat silos and perform their easily mastered tasks. At the same time, they expect their employees to be more creative and inspired. This combination can't succeed.

If we are to transform business, work has to become interesting again, and what could be more fascinating than to interact with people on hot topics like how to tackle never-before-encountered problems or how to complete brand-new types of tasks.

The purpose of **flow** is to set the context for a journey into collective ingenuity and a collaborative response to enterprise needs defined by this novelty.

Flow, the book, emerged from our own work practices. In Fin's case, that was leading high-performing teams that raised the bar in software productivity and business agility. For Haydn, it was working with companies on strategies that were often stalled by the unwillingness of leaders to think differently.

But **Flow** is part of an emerging work ecology. We don't claim to be its inventors.

Flow is an answer to the desire of employees to engage with the same semi-gamified, challenging world they inhabit outside the workplace. In **flow**, roles become fungible again—that is, people are able to take on a wider range of tasks, including the job of continuously designing how work is best done.

People want to be tested at least a little each day; they want continuously to improve their abilities; and to go home with the feeling they did something novel. That means taking on new tasks and responsibilities.

So why does the world of management-thinking persist with the idea that people do not like change?

People are not strangers to change, despite what consultants might tell you. Change is, and always has been, pervasive around us and people embrace it every day of every week.

That smartphone in your pocket (more likely in your hand as you multitask while reading this) did not exist before 2007.

Fifty years ago, people did not eat burgers and drink thickshakes several times a week. In Ireland and the UK people would barely have drunk coffee. There was a time when Starbucks did not exist because nobody needed it.

The Internet in its current form, the World Wide Web, only came into being in 1989 and only really proliferated from about 1996 onwards. Now we access it multiple times daily and have shifted from doing that via computers to accessing it via smartphones and apps (people look at their smartphones around 150 time a day). The app revolution took about three years to sweep the world.

All that is radical change: fast, disruptive and embraced eagerly.

Facebook only became the leader of social networking around 2008. Prior to that, we dabbled with Myspace and Bebo. Around 2006, sharing photos via the web became much easier. Facebook prioritised photo sharing (MySpace limited it) and has been helping us with it ever since. But Snapchat (disappearing photos) has taken a lead, hosting 2.5 billion images each day.

We now take more photos than ever and we share them with a desire nobody knew we had stored up inside us.

All of these activities involve substantial behaviour change. People embrace that just as they embrace adventure sports or e-commerce or mountain bikes.

So do not let anyone kid you that the people in your workplace dislike change. Most of us crave it.

FROM HIERARCHY TO FLOW

In our experience it is business leaders rather than the rest of us who oftentimes find change very hard. Few leaders keep themselves open to new possibilities or trust their own creativity as they climb the organisational ladder. They doubt their ability to deal with the uncertainty that change brings, especially when everyone is looking to see how they will cope.

Most leaders are secretly overwhelmed by the pace of change coming at them. And that's also why many of us who go into work each day continue to face outdated attitudes, deferential hierarchies, efficiency-busting silos, and a lack of momentum to do things differently.

The ability to change should be the very definition of a modern business leader, but sadly so far it is not.

CHANGE STARTS WITH THE LEADER

Here is a cliche: **"Leaders in most organisations need to empower their workforce."**

We know that most organisations need to shift out of hierarchical mode and break down silos. Many are currently sleepwalking into multiple hazards of inefficiency, unaware of how quickly the best performers are increasing the cadence of change. The need for a structural shift is urgent.

But there's a big problem here and to describe it we'll introduce our very first buzzword, cliché, or, as the thesaurus suggests, "bromidic" piece of jargon:

NEGATIVE EMPOWERMENT

This is when people are empowered to do things differently but in a negative context.

There is a negative context to most change. It stems from leaders who talk up empowerment but rubbish the results; or who offer empowerment and then micromanage; or who make oppurtunities seem like a trap. The result is that employee reaction to empowerment is often to see it as a career risk.

A typical leader's diktat is that his or her people need to change in order to meet the needs of the digital age. In these situations there is little reflection on the behavioural changes needed within the leadership group itself. Few leaders say: "Let the change start here". Instead, leaders typically push the problem of change onto their people like bad food they themselves would rather not touch. This is negative empowerment and it is embedded in the mindset of many employees.

Negative empowerment also comes in the form of asking people to feel comfortable with failure. How many times did you read that it is OK to fail, or that as an organisation we need to tolerate failure? Anybody in a position to manage change knows that failure carries serious career risk. People without strong incentives to fail would be dumb to try to do anything other than point themselves in the direction of projects with a high chance of success. They face annual reviews that decide their bonuses.

"But I failed wonderfully this year!" an employee might protest. The sad truth is that failure will count against them unless experimentation is an incentivised part of company culture (as is the case with **flow**).

Another example of negative empowerment is when leaders lock themselves away with consultants to plan a change-management program. change-management is supposed to empower. Like alignment, it is a chimera because you cannot plan and dictate collaboration, engagement, and enthusiasm. You can only frustrate people with those plans.

Real empowerment means employees take over the workplace in some profound way. Simple, no? In all the above cases, three essential ingredients are missing:

Replacement therapy

A replacement for hierarchy, one where responsibility is truly delegated across the entire staff and where people can develop and exercise their own leadership and decision-making skills.

Process ownership

The power and tools to co-create processes that are fluid (i.e., open to change) and therefore adaptive to the needs of the moment. This includes power over workflow design, resource allocation, and decision-making. It is a logical consequence of the first ingredient. A lack of hierarchy can't be created by diktat. The replacement for it has to be designed by the people who inherit power – the employees.

The power of example

Visible change in the character, practices, and relationship skills of leaders.

To put it another way, visual processes, transparency, and a commonly shared representation of work, as advocated in **flow**, keep everyone honest, including the leaders. This is one of the basic principles of **flow**. By making work and work processes visible, we can create a a forum for continuous social interaction and discussion about how best to create value. This is the revolution: employees designing how they will create and deliver value.

When those ingredients aren't in place, workers generally find themselves in a situation where the odds are stacked against them. Negative empowerment can then be the start of a downward spiral in trust and commitment. It is one of the reasons companies squander assets.

THINK LIKE A STARTUP?

Yet, there are significant opportunities for companies that get the new culture of business. One of its defining elements is to think like a startup.

Large enterprises are in fact headed towards startup-like infrastructures. Although we are still a bit vague on this new startup culture, it will become increasingly important, competing with methods such as Agile and Lean.

The advances in IT culture evident in companies like SkyScanner, Etsy, and Paddy Power, and to some degree at Aviva, enable startup activity within a large enterprise. That's a fact.

The reason is that infrastructure is actively being fragmented into smaller packages that can be picked up and assembled like Lego blocks into new business structures. IT is leading the charge.

The conjecture lies in whether or not large companies can create the culture to exploit these new possibilities.

Startups are a helpful place to begin thinking about that. Like everything in business, a simple idea such as "think like a startup" carries important nuances that we would do well not to overlook. The fact is we are headed towards considerably more flexible IT, which can enable startup-like agility. But does that mean really "thinking" like a start up?

There are three reasons for the "think like a startup" mantra being so popular right now, though none may be close enough to what large enterprises really need.

1 Startups can create huge valuations at apparently low cost (a bit of a myth but an interesting one, since many large companies miss out on value creation as they pursue revenues at all cost).

2 Startups are agile (i.e. they can pivot easily), which also makes them quite cheap as a mechanism for broadening the range of innovation.

3 Startups are seen as the key factor in industry sector renewal. Consider, for example, finance, where banks are investing heavily in young upstarts.

Here's a sobering thought, though. In general 50 percent of startups go out of business within five years, and another 40 percent fail to return their investors' money.

That data is fairly historical by now. Newer data from the last five years shows a scarier picture still. In the tech community, 92 percent of startups fail completely within three years, according to the Startup Genome Project, and 74 percent of high-growth internet startups fail due to "premature scaling" or trying to grow too quickly.[3]

Even so, the popularity of incubators and accelerators that try to capture startup culture for large firms is growing.

Companies like Citrix show, with their new accelerator program (called, believe it or not, Startup Accelerator!), that startup culture can stimulate new thinking.

Normally accelerators are external hubs that support startups outside the firm. But Citrix ran its accelerators inside its business lines and found that doing so provoked new ideas in existing teams and exposed the workforce to new ways of working. So, being around startups definitely has value.

Lean is a close cousin of this way of thinking and a friend to startups and large enterprises alike.

LEAN STARTUP

Lean innovation has been well exploited by startups (though we can assume it hasn't reduced the failure rates), spurring large companies to want to try it too.

Lean innovation actually arose in manufacturing,

[3]

The Start Up Genome Project

https://startupgenome. com

where engineers use the principle of continuous small improvements in assembly processes to constantly drive better value. Lean among startups has tended to be more about bringing customers into product-development processes— rather a different need than that of manufacturing. And herein lies the clue to where startups really function well: truly setting out to solve a problem for a customer.

Yet, it is not this attribute that seems to matter most in competitive environments. Continuous, restless improvement is a key to success (and very much at the heart of **flow**). It helped, for example, the Japanese semiconductor industry to dominate areas like display production and computer subcomponents against a supposedly superior U.S. manufacturing industry. It did so by emphasising three things that are not always attributes of startups:

■ Having a willingness (and the systems) to learn quickly.

■ Being only good enough (in the TV industry, Japanese displays were deliberately designed at below par so that there would be fewer valve burnouts).

■ Iterating and improving all the time.

Continuous improvement wins gold medals. We know it is highly efficacious. Yet, in contrast, we are still learning what it takes to make a startup work. The reality is that most startups are not run professionally enough to succeed, which is why they don't survive.

The majority of startups are therefore surely a very poor model for how a large company can work, whether it uses lean processes or not. In fact, the kind of startups that enterprises need to learn from are very rare. You'll know them by these characteristics:

■ A desire to find and solve problems.

■ Hence a period of consolidated discovery (maybe as long as two years) to be sure they have the right product or service before they can begin to grow.

■ Being inherently curious and hypothesising all the time about next steps.

■ The ability to curate sufficient amounts of the right resources (e.g., cash, goodwill, people, tech infrastructure) for very rapid growth.

■ Being fungible, in the sense that roles become interchangeable and labour is not divided in traditional ways (in effect the division of labour has become a handicap).

- Some tangible engagement with customers early on.

- Extraordinary adaptability in the approach to IT architecture and the capacity to adopt cutting-edge technologies and concepts as and when new ways of working evolve.

- A tireless commitment to continuous innovation day in and day out.

- A workforce incentivised by significant share ownership or a higher purpose.

- An unusual ability to listen and learn, which ensures they don't get ahead of themselves.

In order to replicate successful startup culture, large companies need all these characteristics as well as hugely ambitious goals and a sense of purpose beyond just making money.

When Fin, for example, was CTO at Paddy Power, the $5 billion online betting company, he led a team that facilitated **7 million price changes every Saturday afternoon.**

Think about that. Isn't it incredible? Paddy Power could not only change its prices, though. It also had to create products on the fly. As, say, a soccer game proceeded, many factors could unexpectedly change: the weather might turn, managers could make substitutions, a star player might get injured, and pitches could deteriorate. Paddy Power was able to offer new bets over the whole course of a game, depending on the position of play on the pitch, weather conditions, players around the ball, pitch conditions, progress of the match, the referee, and many more factors. They would do this across all the league games and, more or less in the same breath, do the same for tennis and golf.

Large companies need those kinds of ambitions and capabilities.

To be successful at this, they also need a workflow that delegates decision-making power to those close to the daily action of doing business (like the brokers who devised the bets that drew people into Paddy Power). Without that delegation, you can have great technology but no business to speak of.

Now, put the startup culture to one side, large companies often have to make very big decisions, usually multimillion-dollar ones, on the back of insufficient data. Executives often have to play a hunch in a way startups will never experience. That's the nature of business—taking a risk.

The big boys are not just scaling a new idea, like a startup does, nor can they always iterate a minimum viable product (the goal of Lean). Instead, they will often need to turn a big ship in a small space. Place big bets. Use their muscle.

The experience of large enterprises and high-growth startups might actually converge around this one point. They experience a similar problem around scale.

Their core issue is how to balance risk with the responsibility that goes with having access to significant resources, such as VC cash or a positive decision from a board. The difficult job, then, is to scale an opportunity and this is inherently a process problem.

This, actually, is the moment when most startups fail. They go under when they have money to grow. In a sense, the startup fails when it reaches the position a large company often finds itself in, which is having a new product, resources, and the ambition to scale.

The challenges of expanding a market are behind many of the decisions a large company has to make. Neither they nor the startup understands well enough how to go about getting decisions right at this stage.

Take Google's attempt to create a product called Glass, a heads up display baked into more or less normal glasses. With **Glass** Google effectively became something like a Kickstarter-funded startup. They persuaded software developers to pay $1,500 for a combination of the software development kit to write to Glass and a pair of beta Glasses that developers could experiment with.

Yet Glass failed. The world's most innovative company failed at being a startup!

Glass hurt Google's reputation for getting good outcomes once the company ditched the product (but not for long, because by then it was promising to give the world a giant AI brain, and yes, everyone went along with that one too). The baton of wearable social networking, however, now passed to the new generation of startup companies like SNAP, not the incumbents Google and Facebook.

As we mentioned before, most companies fail when they secure the resources to scale up, not when they are in the early phase of testing the market. It seems that resources are a company's worst enemy.

The literature on entrepreneurship suggests that people who succeed have what is called "effectual" qualities. In this context, read that as "the ability to secure the wide range of assets needed for success".

By and large, these are not cash. They are assets like belief and loyalty, having people who will go the extra mile for you, being the guy who holds things together.

So then, the startup qualities that matter for large companies are not easy to master nor are they easy to facilitate. We'll look at those qualities overleaf.

Precisely what is the right culture for an innovative firm is truly complex. It has some startup elements but we can't ignore the problems faced by leaders whose world is changing around them. Some of the problems are near to being intractable for current leadership skills:

Managing process model innovation; increasing innovation to address new customer segments and needs; introducing transformational technology like AI, IoT, distributed ledger; contemplating global economic restructuring. This is a handful!

There is a new way to address complexity but we should not expect it to be simple. It is a combination of approaches that we will walk you through in this book such as harnessing collective intelligence (which we define differently from most people's version. We mean using social interaction to funnel all the knowledge that people pick up in the course of work and social networking); breaking work down into smaller chunks to identify where real value lies and to reduce risk, reducing cycle time (the time it takes to finish a task) to a day or two; visualising all work so that social interaction has context and a venue; and process model co-creation, all help to convert the workplace to a creative and vibrant venue.

In particular the relationship between a Customer Wall that identifies new segments, products or features to work on and the Executive Portfolio Wall, which creates a more rational executive investment strategy, are critical to your success.

Going back briefly to the startup, when all said and done, what distinguishes the great ones is good social interaction where flawed thinking is exposed and where loyalty is only rewarded in the event of success.

Creating the conditions for good social interaction is within your grasp.

GETTING THE *RIGHT* THINGS DONE

One of the prizes we want you to take away from this book is a new way of looking at the meaning and organisation of change, because highly desirable, new, enterprise-startup qualities lie deep in the concept of **flow**.

To get to **flow** it is important to recognise that significant change is usually mismanaged. In fact good change is impossible to manage in any conventional sense because it has to be co-created. The needs of today's firms will only be met if executives invite employees into the continuous definition of how to get work done in ways that create real value.

In place of this we hear that recurrent but simplistic mantra "the right to fail". In reality nobody has a right to fail. We can all make mistakes but the whole point of work is to find ways to steer us towards success. The right to fail mantra is a cop out for people who don't understand the new needs of the enterprise.

A case in point: A leading institution we were talking to recently had a significant new technology it wanted to develop and implement. After spending $3 million it was clear to the leadership team that the chosen solution was a complete dud. The "pivot" to a different solution took another $6 million. Curiously, almost everybody on the initial project knew from early on that they were baking up a disaster. This is a very common scenario in enterprises that mandate change through fiat and technology. Nobody had a strong enough voice to prevent the failure from unfolding. As millions of dollars went down the drain, leaders were forced to say: We all have the right to fail as part of our new culture. That helped people to save face. Nonetheless, nobody ended that project happy and nobody wanted to add up the losses.

The overspend and embarrassment could have been avoided using a co-creation system where more voices were given air time, as of right. That is **flow.** The right to be heard, which is far more powerful than the right to fail.

Co-creating change, and having the capacity to design new work processes quickly, means that leaders have less and less power to impose monolithic solutions.

That begs the question:

What is the real purpose of a leader?

We will say a fair bit about that later on but the basic principle is that leaders are there to set the conditions for good social interaction, where they harness the intelligence of the group and direct it towards continuous improvement in products, services, and processes.

Change of this type, though, is ultimately dependent on how people react to the need for continuous learning. Surprisingly, there are very few ways to absorb information (create it through feedback, learn by rote/repetition, or adopt a belief over time). But what we are seeking is not one of those traditional learning mechanisms.

In our new age of work, learning is, or should be, a product of group interaction. In an empowered organisation, learning is about the group interacting well to produce good results, then reflecting on its actions as it refines its understanding of the work processes and tools that got it to a good outcome.

In other words, learning is a process of co-creation.

In contrast to this nirvana, we are currently in one of two uncomfortable learning positions at work:

Personal silos

We incessantly hold up our paws to the keyboard as we sit in our cubicles and stare at a computer screen learning from a video, a report or a spreadsheet, with little capacity to actually speak to people.

Groupies

We are constantly in meeting rooms where we are caught in the headlights of consensus-forming tedium or listening to a manager who knows it all. The majority are deterred from speaking freely because of the overwhelming desire to appear "aligned" with the organisation's goals or an aggressive leader or a deferential team.

None of these forms of learning allows enterprises to capture the benefits of the group's ingenuity and wisdom in the way successful startups can. Nor do they benefit from new infrastructure (web, cloud, microservices) that is pushing great companies towards extraordinary levels of flexibility in their operations, decision-making and capacity to improve like a startup.

Screens and meeting rooms do not liberate the majority of people's talents.

We advocate entirely new work conditions: WALLS, not cubicles. WALLS as meeting places. Hypotheses, conversations and open debate should take place in public at Walls.

Cubicles are places to hide. Meetings are for dozing off. WALLS are large-scale visualisations that become the focal points for social interaction about work and process design. They are common property in the company, formed and managed by employees, with leaders looking on in order to shape conversations about value.

Walls are places for people to congregate. They are visual representations of workflow, of tools to use or discard, project breakdowns, idea flows in and out of projects, risks, issues, evaluations, customer insights, reflections, lessons, games, jokes, wishes, and congratulations. Put simply, they are large flat surfaces backed by bricks and mortar, with an internal surface that surrounds an office. Used properly they can help people share the practice of creating a work process and doing a job together. They represent the opportunity to reinvent work as fluid rather than fixed processes.

The need for fluidity is simple:

"It is now very hard to develop expertise and value through the repetition of tasks."

**Adam Smith's Ghost
(a.k.a. Fin Goulding and Haydn Shaughnessy)**

THE ERRORS OF SMITH

Adam Smith, the father of economics as we know it, thought that the micro-division of labour was the key to productivity. He thought this for three reasons:

- Good old repetition is efficient (do a task often enough and it becomes automatic).

- Continuity breeds familiarity (no switching between tasks and relearning).

- A specialised worker gains insights into their tasks and this leads to better working methods and innovation.

In the 18th century and maybe for the 250 years that followed, the Adam Smith dictum of specialisation worked every well.

That way of learning is over, Adam.

Today, we need people who can take on tasks nobody has ever attempted before.

Like what?

How about all those social-media campaigns that cropped up after 2007. Some folks had to invent and deliver them. Or the application of AI? How about the possibility of distributed ledger technology and the Internet of Things. DevOps, the integration of development, testing and operational tasks in IT?

As we rapidly apply large-scale ambient computing for the first time in human history, many, many tasks are entirely new. And they require new work processes.

Here's two salient facts about these new tasks:

1 There is no opportunity to apply Adam Smith's logic and do them 100 times a day. At most, they're performed once or twice ever in one person's career. Case in point: Google's adoption process for AI involves 300 major steps. That's 300 new skills that have to be learned and will only be applied by most people on the one or two occasions that their company implements an AI.

2 By the time we learn to routinise many of these skills, they are already outdated. Specialisation cannot keep up with the fast flow of change.

Process experimentation and co-design is becoming an emergent property of work for those reasons. When you have domains with 300 new steps, you cannot go to the trouble of dividing out the tasks in a Smithian way. You need people to agree what to do right now, next, and later in the day, with the understanding that you will face tasks you've never before encountered (and you may soon be part of a team delivering hundreds of improvements in the next, say, sixty minutes). In these circumstances, you have to make up the method to suit the task in hand.

Your colleagues are in the same boat: everyone is tackling a new problem and everybody goes back to being a craft worker, or maker, those artisans that Smith's theories consigned to the dustbin of history. The only methodology available to you is communications, and you cannot communicate effectively by looking into a screen. What you have instead is **flow.** It dictates that you have to go to the WALL and interact.

Haydn's first job was in an abattoir. One day, a man with a knife said, "It's all about the pig."
But it's not about the pig or the one thing you have to do repetitively. It's about the people around you.

Providing the right formats for interaction, setting the tone, building trust, creating and sustaining confidence, accepting the emotional burden of other people's belief in you—these are the orchestration skills that leaders need if they are to set the scene for good social interaction at work. They need these skills to make their organisations successful.
In fact, everyone needs them. Change grows from emergent behaviours, and it is our role and responsibility to guide what is emerging.

NOT NUDGE

Now, it may seem as though we are simply proposing something along the lines of nudge theory.

We are not.

For those not familiar with it, nudge theory suggests that significant positive change can be brought about by good micro-interventions—that is, offering people small encouragements to act differently rather than legislating a change in behaviour.

The classic example of nudge is the fly etched into men's urinals to get monsieur to aim properly. No amount of telling men to be hygienic works. Give them something to aim at, however, and the problem is solved.

There is nothing wrong with that kind of minimalist approach, depending on your objectives. One of the secrets to winning those diamond-studded spectacles we mentioned earlier, though, is to be self directed (:-)). The dynamic in work has to be about our agency and what we can achieve in redefining, continuously, how we solve problems. This has to happen in the rapid flow of work as we try to serve a wider range of customers with better and more features, products, and services. We can only address the new world of novelty by taking small steps together.

Big businesses, however, are usually tempted to take big steps because they need "transformation," or a complete overhaul in how they function. In reality, big steps just end up creating a lot of barriers. They get in the way of how we actually need to work in today's very dynamic, difficult, and competitive economy. That's why nudge became so important.

But to repeat, **flow** is not nudge. **Flow** is all about turning social interaction into good decision-making.

Everything we will write about comes back to that idea.

Flow puts human interaction at the heart of change. It says (we say), "The social interactions that make up our workday are the setting for good decisions that add value."

This is important because while other methods, like Agile, can help you work fast, and methods like nudge can improve behaviours, they don't help you decide what is good work and what is bad work. They will force you to plan too far ahead, whereas social interaction, within a very visible process (the WALL), forces you to keep big plans at arm's length. **Flow** replaces formal planning with eyeballs trained on the problems at hand. Agile might be run by smart or dumb people but **flow** is out there for everyone to see, comment on, criticise, and hypothesise around. It is collective intelligence graffiti and most importantly it works.

Fin Goulding

Fin is a CITO, but of course that role doesn't exist. In fact, he switches between CIO (Chief Information Officer) and CTO (Chief Technology Officer) depending on which challenge he faces. For instance, fixing the gaps in a startup when it scales too quickly or redeeming the sins of the past when a large corporation outsources too much. He's been a technologist for many years and has pioneered new ways of working at places like Paddy Power and now as Aviva's International CIO, leading teams across the Americas, Europe and India. He is a member of the senior leadership team, dragging a 300-year-old company into the digital age. Aviva Ireland is a test bed, a lighthouse for the wider group and an organisation that Fin is helping to disrupt itself.

Before that, he worked as CTO at lastminute.com, running a large offshore centre as a CIO in Argentina. He was also the SVP of Technology for Visa in the U.S. He hates taking the same route to work more than two days running. Talking of running, he's obsessive about it and competes in at least four marathons a year. This gives him the time to think and be creative.

Fin has a burning desire to describe a new framework that goes beyond Agile and captures what really happens when large organisations get serious about change.

The **flow** principles we will outline later in the book stem from Fin's adaptation of Agile working methods and lean innovation and Haydn's work on ecosystem strategy.

WHO ARE WE?

Haydn Shaughnessy

Haydn is one of the world's leading experts in innovation and transformation. From his early 20s on, he has been studying how economies change and analysing large scale disruption.

He began doing this kind of work in the 1990s at the European Commission in Brussels. There, he was part of an ARPA-like team tasked with finding ways for Europe to come out on top in the race for leadership in mobile phones. Before there was broadband, he was working on broadband applications. Before 3G he was trying to figure out what broader bandwidth in mobile would mean for applications. One area he worked on was "communities of interest" or what are now called social networks. Before that he worked in broadcasting as the television industry transitioned from film to video and automated newsrooms.

He works with organisations on the challenges of disruption and routes to durable transformation and is a leading expert in platform economics.

He has developed a variety of ways of measuring innovation and change. Part of this work involves describing ways in which rigid human systems can become more fluid, the meeting point between his and Fin's work.

Flow and fluidity are two sides of the same coin: work methods and management outlook.

But that's the philosophy. The book will also deliver something very concrete: specific ways to make change easier and tools you can use to become more productive when taking on the big challenges of the day.

Making it work in practice

1. THE CUSTOMER WALL

Thinking Like A Startup:
A Method for the Larger Company

There is something unusually daunting about taking the first steps into any new activity or mindset. Even the great French chef Auguste Escoffier had to peel his first onion somewhere, somehow, one day.

To remodel your thinking and work flow is unusually hard, as we said above. But let's get started anyway. One of the most significant steps you can make is to create a more fluid market segmentation. Most companies segment simply. They use demographics (age groups), gender, and income. But today we can know so much more about customers. And if you don't care to find out the range of services they want then a crafty start up will.

We should all be experimenting with ways to get customers more front of mind. In Fin's case, that means a new customer lab; for Haydn, it is what he calls the Customer WALL (though he picked up the idea from Fin, who is really the chief visualisation guru).

Businesses have a crying need for new customer segmentation techniques. Even good companies take a naive view of who their customer is. They use personas, or caricatures of the customer in place of anything rooted in reality.

In one bank we spoke with recently the customer segmentation was between regular account holders and high net worth individuals! Two segments? This lack of attention to who the customer is provides the entry point for a startup to steal market share. It leaves the company wide open to the startup community, which rightly obsesses over who is not being properly served by incumbents.

Short story: Haydn walked into the office of a major bank who have emblazoned on the wall of their reception area, "Customers First". There were some other homilies about serving them, too. But as he walked the corridors of this bank, there were no customers to be seen and no doubt they would have felt welcome, anyway. There were no pictures, other than expensive artwork, and no map to show where customers were located. Nor any reflection of customer activity on social media.

Customer First is a myth until the day you invite customers in and the **Customer WALL** is a way to bring their stories and interests inside the organisation's physical space.

So to start, here is a simple visual method for creating a customer focus that will help you think like a startup, though maybe one that exists in large organisations and is currently dormant. It visualises customer needs. By the way, it is meant to be fun!

There are really five steps to it:

1 Creating a new market segmentation based on customers' whole range of interests.

2 Finding representative customers who are active online.

3 Creating the imagery of both the segments and customers.

4 Inviting employees to understand the product-market fit.

5 Iterating ideas that are relevant to customers' needs but are missing.

To do this you need the following elements:

- The Customer WALL.
- StatSocial social-media data.
- Paper.li to collect opinion from around the web.
- Cards or extra sticky Post-it Notes.
- A scrapbook.
- Somebody who loves curating information.

Do you have a space somewhere prominent where you can begin sticking up cards of your company's Twitter followers? Maybe a screen where you can feed their Twitter posts, Pinterest images, or even Snapchat memories? A wall that people can't miss?

You are not aiming for perfection. The goal here is to get a good enough representation of what is going on with your customers, enough that you can iterate over time.

Segmentation and ecosystems

Get access to tools like StatSocial, where CEO Michael Hussey has created an incredible data resource from over 600 million Twitter accounts. He tracks those users across 45 social-media platforms to create anonymised breakdowns of, say, what additional brands Tide customers like or what people who prefer Samsung Gear watch on the TV.

This breakdown gives you two invaluable assets:

1 You begin to understand what your customers like in addition to your products—they like you and real estate or marketing or photography.

2 You get a sense of where your customer ecosystem lies and how it is structured. In each of these segments there are smaller companies and potential partners to help serve customers better. That could be the basis of a new strategy.

Post a few cards on the wall with what you see as your customers' real priorities and mix of interests (drawn from social-media analysis), what new segments they fall into, and where there might be an underserved need.

The tool we use, StatSocial is not cheap but for a dive into who your customers really are, how they naturally segment, and what interests they are engaged with, it is unmissable.

Social media gives you access to customers' concerns, interests, and hates, and also their photographs. Print those out. Stick them to cards or simply pin them to the Wall under the heading "Our Customers." Get somebody who looks organised enough to do a daily update and a monthly clear down of extracts from customer Twitter accounts. Nothing dramatic but a start.

Create an Innovation column next to these customer segments where you can document how to make their lives better. Given what you know about these customers and learn about them each day, how can you hack around with products and services to improve value?

Curate a Paper.li that reflects the views of your customers, streaming information in from Twitter and Pinterest. Circulate. Play around with tools like this (you may already subscribe to Sprinklr for example).

Encourage people to engage by organising a standup or two specifically on what these walls mean. The purpose is to create interaction and conversation.

Your *Customer Innovation Wall* will have:

- The market segmentation
- The actual customers
- Ideas that relate directly to their interests

People should feel free to comment (leave a felt-tip pen handy) and they should be welcome to add to it.

You may be wondering what all this amounts to? Are we simply saying learn more about customers? Well that's no bad thing. But actually when you see the range of things customers are interested in as well as your own products you can create a well structured segmentation that doesn't rely on gender, demographics or income.

Your segmentation will be structured around behaviour. In the car industry, for example, many people who follow Ford are also fond of Bill Gates and wine. This says something about the aspirational nature of a non-premium brand. Women are especially likely to follow Ford's after-sales service tweets. Many people who like Ford cars also like bicycles. Here is a new segmentation in the making, giving new clues as to the overall make up of a customer base.

There are other ways to use customer walls. Fin uses a Customer Issues Wall. There is a version of it positioned in the office entrance where everyone can see the issues customers are having with the company's products.

Creating a Customer WALL is a start towards making innovation relevant. But it has to fit within a wider picture of transformation. What we aim for is to create segmentations that can inspire very targeted innovation ideas or new partnerships to address new and unmet needs.

HOW THE DIGITAL WORLD CREATED NEW NEEDS

BEFORE WE GO INTO THE SPECIFICS OF *FLOW*, LET'S CONSIDER THE EMERGING NUANCES—AND ABRUPT CHANGES—CREATED BY A DIGITAL SOCIETY.

In the late 2000s, as the full impact of the 2008 financial crisis became obvious, I, Haydn, was headed towards the border police at Munich airport. Like all things in Germany, the airport is vast, including the number of border guards.

The guard I headed towards seemed to be doubled over in pain. But as I approached, it became obvious that, no, he just had his head over a smartphone and was texting. He waved me by without even glancing at my passport. And Munich isn't the only place I've encountered this: I see police texting in between scanning passports at almost every airport I visit.

This is a remarkable example of behaviour change. The devices these border guards use now link around 4 billion people—2 billion of them owners of smartphones and the rest owners of feature phones.

That means that suddenly, if you are in the business of providing services, you have a market that is several billion people strong. The people in this market can love you, ignore you or challenge you. More than likely, before they buy from any company today, they will ask others what they think. They are the enterprise's hardest-working and best marketers.

This complex situation has led to many important

changes but let's try to summarise them in a few stages: access, expectation, real-time, scale and intelligence. While these are important drivers of change, there is one more and it is critical. **Speed**.

Behind the scenes, and unknown to many CEOs, the pace of change is reaching lightspeed, particularly in the IT shop where DevOps and microservices are breaking down old enterprise IT infrastructures and creating the possibility of much more autonomy, much more capacity to mix and match the software capabilities of the firm to new business opportunities. This will be crucial to an enterprise's ability to be truly agile.

Speed also shapes these five steps:

Access

People now shop or access information from anywhere and at any time. As an example, take finance. Your old financial broker used to dispense wisdom on equity investments at his office between the hours of 9 and 5. He now needs an infrastructure that allows you to access information and potentially execute financial trades at any time, from anywhere.

This is known as the **Amazon Effect**, and few industries are immune to this state of being always on, instantly responsive and operating at scale, yet also being as personal as it gets. This has put pressure on suppliers.

To return to our finance example, companies like Fidelity provide background infrastructure that allows customers 24/7 access to their investment products. The investment industry used to rely on brokers or "middlemen" who advised clients on their portfolios. But today, the effect of pervasive real-time information is that:

- Many people know as much or more than the old intermediary.

- They want to transact when the intermediary is out to dinner or tucked up in bed.

- Therefore old distribution models are coming under intense strain.

In addition, if a service provider fails to make services available 24/7, the frustration this causes to customers will spur a startup somewhere to solve that problem. Access and Amazon. It is game changing, structurally so.

Expectation

People expect such access to operate at a very high level of execution, with no clumsy interfaces and certainly no downtime. Add to that brilliant customer service, slicker marketing that doesn't patronise audiences, deft use of interactive channels like Facebook and Pinterest, and a presence everywhere (TV, newspapers, outdoor, social-media channels).

Companies are scrambling to create this new kind of platform capability while also keeping up with the pace of customers' demands.

Most consumers do not want to be told what they can or cannot do and most have so much to occupy their time that companies who want to get and retain their attention are finding it ever harder.

The world of computing, whether it's for sales, marketing, or record keeping, was built as if every user was a computing expert. These assumptions introduced acute usability issues. Slowly, slowly, the online world is being designed around people who actually don't use traditional computing systems, who don't want to know anything about them and just want to shop, search, share, or show off via mobile phones.

Real-time

The enormous and unprecedented connectivity of people across the globe is one contributing factor in the move towards a real-time economy. Platforms now have users numbering in the billions who connect any time, in any place. These users range over many different services, apps, or products. The platforms that serve them are highly scaled but also offer a broad scope of products and services in what is now known as the long tail.

All this contributes to a business environment where ever-more decisions have to be made quickly across a wider range of activity.

We already mentioned the online travel company SkyScanner is expecting to make thousands of software releases in its systems every day, with each requiring a decision somewhere along the line (if only in how groups of decisions can be automated). Such a colossal rate of change will become the norm. At the same time, the need to automate innovation is also becoming the standard, so that companies never get caught napping (or never get caught between silos). This too spurs on the need for new process design.

In a recent survey of executives responsible for innovation, we found that the pressure to do effective AI, for example, came from the need to delegate decisions—instantly—to people further down the hierarchy. In other words, companies need processes that enable real-time decision-making.

Scale

An inescapable part of the modern economy is

the scale of activities companies can now manage successfully. But most executives still do not think correctly about this. We already mentioned Fin's work at Paddy Power, where his team enabled 7 million price changes each Saturday afternoon.

This may sound like an incredible technical feat but stated like that, it's **only** a technical feat. IT at its best but so what?

In reality, the consequence of this incredible scale is that anyone involved—salespeople at Paddy Power, brokers, those framing the bets and interacting with the public—suddenly had to master a whole new pace of work. Processes like this change work-life entirely and make traditional planning practically impossible.

Go back a generation and today's throughput on systems like Paddy Power's was unimaginable. Traditionally, companies were expected to run into diminishing marginal returns as they grew. At a given point, every extra dollar spent would yield less of a return. Most systems had limited endpoint-management capability. They were designed to manage, say, 100,000 customer accounts at most.

Today there is no limit to scale. And the good news is that scale is not hampered by extraordinary capital costs that suppress profitability. Scale can be achieved flexibly in the Cloud.

Intelligence

To deliver access that will meet consumers' high level of expectation and in real-time, we are now in a race to create more AI systems that can give us better insights and also help us automate decision processes.

Mindjet, who make mind mapping and innovation-management software, are working on systems that will allow, say, cars to report on the relative performance of different engine and braking systems. That data can feed into an innovation program to prioritise where company resources are best spent. It's innovation automated.

GE also believe that, in time, the human element of the innovation process will disappear. Taking automated innovation a step further, their argument is that cars, as a population, will inform systems on what to innovate on their behalf but that could mean the assembly line needs an extra capability, for example, to fit an additional part. A 3D printer will automatically add that capability. Machines will burnish the capabilities of other machines, all in response to data.

Superficially AI is not currently sophisticated. We are building it into customer interfaces in a bid to save spending on human labour, a very traditional use of innovation. Underneath this surface-level application, companies like Amazon, CISCO, Microsoft, Alibaba and Google are embedding intelligent systems into the infrastructure of communications: machines will sell parts and provide services to each other, maybe even negotiating the price based on one machine's current capacity and backlog. They will most certainly log the transaction, probably onto a blockchain.

In ten years' time, there will be infinitely less friction in the way services function around us because of automated negotiation. To reach that point, many of the divisions of work within organisations will have to be merged, since the advantage of digital comes from not having to hand over work from one stage to another. In fact, people will be written out of work and will have to find knowledge-based alternatives.

Companies that are succeeding with these changes come in two varieties:

1 The tech giants that have defined the infrastructure for scale and velocity.

2 High-growth startups that are very capable of adopting the infrastructure as it evolves.

We already pointed out, in the last chapter, the characteristics that define these companies. Perhaps the most important is that they avoid silos—especially any divisions between the technical capabilities that create scale and the capabilities that create markets.

Marketing is often built into the design of the overall business platform and the process of doing rapid innovation delivery. That means CMOs need to become more adept at using digital technology. Many admin tasks—payroll, simple accounting—will be outsourced to a platform that can perform them far more efficiently. The company can instead focus on our favorite triumvirate, scale, scope, and speed, along with a few new friends:

■ **Scaling** its operational capability.

■ Broadening the **scope** of its offer.

■ Doing so at **speed**.

■ Enhancing the capabilities of its people.

■ Creating a learning model that allows it to innovate continuously.

All this creates one final need: options building. When working at speed in fast-changing markets, companies need to create more options for themselves. They need to innovate in advance, before the need for a new product becomes apparent and to be willing to spend on options that might never hit the market. As we said earlier, they need to do a whole lot more with their resources.

MICROSERVICES AND THE END OF BIG SYSTEMS

To quickly recap, today's systems have to provide 24/7 access to services, meet high expectations of quality, take place at scale, scope and speed and provide an opportunity for introducing intelligence and automation. With all those requirements, companies need more than the conventional rhythm of work activities to do business. By the same token enterprises need a culture that can profit from a post-agile age.

Most organisations have gone some way towards implementing Agile development techniques. They are also likely to use Lean methods. The idea that innovation can and should be done as cheaply as possible has taken hold along with these new work methods as we all seek to innovate more and faster at low cost.

Along with it, though, should come the realisation that a lot of what passes for innovation is just wasted effort. We do a lot that is fast and cheap but maybe the reason for that is that we have poor innovation methods. We implement projects often without first asking if the objectives themselves are really necessary or if the process of achieving them is actually efficient in delivering real value.

Here's another way of putting that: You can do great Agile but being agile doesn't guarantee a good output. It only assures you of a reasonably fast one compared to what went before.

In order to secure value consistently we need to rethink our objectives and techniques at a very fast cadence. Agile does not address this need and Lean iteration is just too slow.

There is no decision process capable of addressing the need other than one that allows the people doing the work to assess the value of outputs as they become apparent. The call on whether to stop or speed up innovation has to be made at the coalface. This is almost a definition of empowerment.

This is too radical for many companies. Not only do most of them get held back by dreadful silos—for example between IT and marketing or leaders and the rest of us—but, reality check here, many processes within an enterprise are actually there to support siloed working as opposed to supporting efficiency, velocity, or innovation (see our views on the HR burden below).

In the end, organisations pitch us all into silos because we are incentivised by our wage packets to burrow down into the smallest possible silo—the silo of you or me against everyone else. Agile has not helped this

miasma of dysfunction.

To some degree, the principles of agility have spread to other parts of an organisation from the IT shop. Marketers, admins, and even the CFO's office are increasingly interested in how to make decisions faster, work outside traditional planning constraints, and be more responsive.

But much of this is not Agile methodology. Let's look closer.

In essence, Agile is associated with three major goals:

1 To move software development closer to customers in order to work iteratively with them to capture their needs. This is the starting point for continuous customer feedback-loops that signal when we need to accelerate, slow down, or pivot projects.

2 To allow software teams to bring different elements of the old waterfall process together, as happens with DevOps (the merging of development, testing and operations, often with business analysts and business owners rolled in). This not just a much slicker way to

build software, it is actually a model for how the new enterprise needs to function because it relies on fungible roles and it reduces handovers. It is the movement that began the job of turning Adam Smith's division of labour dictums upside down. Interestingly Devops is not Agile but it has emerged in parallel.

3 To support the idea of visible work. That usually means visualisations like Scrum or Kanban boards that get a limited range of brain work (planning, coding, integrating) out into the open where it can be seen, shared, judged, critiqued, and changed. More often than not, this is managed by an IT director.

Agile is not without its problems, though. These tend to be fourfold:

Innovation overload

In the modern enterprise, the hunger for innovation often creates a kind of delirium. There are too many new ideas and requests, too much time being used to add very little value, and an inability to put a stop to the waste because decision-making is still detached from processes. This is partly a result of Agile and Lean, not to mention the daft idea that doing "fail fast, fail cheap" is the same as doing good work. It isn't. It can be, if you have delegated decision-making and you have continuous evaluation of projects. But those qualities are rare.

The lack of an options approach

Resources are always limited and the development process needs better and faster ways to identify new functions, features, and products that add value to the business. Companies typically lack the insight or desire to create a range of options that can be rolled into development programmes. Agile doesn't help here.

The influence of traditional planning

Agile isn't really a method or framework for designing a work process. Work under Agile still needs, and gets, a grand plan if the CIO/CTO is to allocate resources efficiently. That bakes rigidity into what work gets done, with the priority being speed rather than creating options or clarifying value. This sprint system (two- to three-week cycles of work) is just too long and creates too many problems when you have to integrate dozens of updates per day.

Lack of real implementation

Many aspects of the Agile manifesto are great but are not implemented. Instead, IT shops convert Agile into a way of making grand plans happen faster without challenging IT's culture of rigidity.

In the absence of a new framework for workflow design, two things are happening:

You get the very valuable trend towards DevOps and microservices, which is to break everything up into smaller packages and a focus on what it takes to stitch the work of many small teams together. This is exciting stuff that can be adopted by any department. It can be done under the Agile banner, though it is an important departure.

Or you get waterfall by accident: Very large projects that just happen to get done in quick sprints, which is what Agile is all about.

The world of DevOps and microservices is much different from Agile and Lean. The unique asset they bestow on the organisation is the capacity to merge many of the IT, marketing, and business functions into teams that enjoy a constant view of what customers are responding to and how therefore to direct and manage continuous improvement.

The upside of this is that people become very astute in practising the art of real-time planning. Like the detailed work breakdown that goes with it, this is a new skill for most, and, when handled sensitively, poses precisely the kind of challenge that gets people excited about coming into work. It is by default a social process where people have to talk and consult each other about:

- What work should get done (which has most value to customers).
- What the most promising solutions might be.
- How that work is best executed.
- What the governance process should be (what can be changed, what people need permission to do).

As you can see, we are big fans of topics such as DevOps and microservices. The latter lets us eat the complex technical elephant that normally overwhelms software teams. DevOps is the integration of processes that allows teams to deliver with optimum efficiency.

Job done?

Well, not really. This book has a much larger theme. The word "continuous" has many connotations in work, and we have tried to bring all these together. As well as continuous delivery, or DevOps, there is continuous learning and continuous improvement, two needs that have been around a long time but haven't always got an adequate hearing. And there is continuous experimentation and continuous process design.

Meanwhile, DevOps and microservices are offering a new way to view the capacity of firms. Beyond what technologists love about them, they present an opportunity to create real agility because the size of work is smaller.

In effect, it is not Agile that is creating real agility. DevOps, and particularly microservices, are changing the fundamental relationship between a firm and its markets.

There are three exciting possibilities emerging as IT refocuses its methods in a way that is infinitely more business-centric than it ever was:

Better predictions of value

Microservices create an environment where business people can write the rules for how software behaves. As the software is small and adaptive there are more opportunities to generate data about how these packages are used and in turn to abstract this data into a visual representation that shows the interaction between different services as we deliver value to the customer. This is allowing us to simulate the interaction of many services before we build them out.

Holistic teams

DevOps requires hybrid or holistic teams, with product owners and business analysts sitting alongside developers, testers and operational team members. This is the ultimate structure to address inefficient hand-offs and to drive collaboration between business and IT. Could this signal the end for the term IT? Are we seeing work silos collapsing and new ways of working emerge?

Operating like a startup

The promised land is nigh! As we break down large software infrastructure into many small components, will it lead to large companies being able to create mini-startups, rapidly deploying a subset of services within huge enterprises but in the form of a quickly compiled new business? Technology certainly allows for such a scenario. The jury is out, though, on where it will lead. One thing is for sure: continuous evolution is going strong.

Advocating for these principles and opportunities across the whole organisations is what **flow** is all about. It is the culture that helps technology eliminate the silos between doers and decision makers. It should also eliminate the silos between departments.

It builds on DevOps and microservices as a method, principle, or architecture and extends it to the enterprise as a whole. But its defining feature is this: total flow of work and decisions from the customer and executive suite, right down to the point of delivering new services and continuously improving them

SOCIAL BUSINESS OR VISIBLE WORK?

Which value system will support these changes? For a decade now we have worked with many variants of social business (Enterprise 2.0, E2.0, social business itself). Big companies are used to buying big systems and have embraced the opportunity to instal them in the E2.0 space. In keeping with that thinking, many of them have also bought social-business platforms like Quad (from Cisco) or IBM's Connections.

This betrays a typical misstep in solving a serious productivity problem.

In theory, people are supposed to communicate and collaborate more when they use social-business platforms because they can text coworkers and view stream-of-consciousness newsfeeds.

Unfortunately, these big systems are usually expensive, overdesigned, hard to use, and involve too much learning. Even worse, they can create additional silos, as those who understand the technology quickly become super-users and the rest watch (or as we used to say in netspeak, **lurk**).

We are opponents of social-business platforms for those very reasons. It is not helpful to shoehorn people into more online systems. People need to get up and talk. However, it is obvious that there is no technology or platform that allows for that, no such thing as a conversation vendor. Bizarrely, real interaction between people sinks down the corporate agenda in the absence of a system or a platform.

Technology cannot address the key issues of social interaction: managing the belief systems that make people happy at work and providing the liberty to co-create in a genuinely empowered office.

An important potential solution emerged about a decade ago: visible work. At the same time as the vendor community got lucky with social platforms, the idea of visible work wound its way through blogs and other sinews in the communications web. It has had a hard time getting the attention it deserves.

Most work right now is invisible because knowledge workers hold it in their heads but the potential for visible work has been overshadowed by techniques like the Wiki.

Over the past decade, wikis have become a popular way of getting what's in your head onto a page you share with other people. These are pretty useful in their own way (as a system of record) but, like social-business platforms, they still do more to inhibit than promote social interaction. And it is not at all clear that they produce value for all the effort that goes into them.

A far more effective technology exists. We call it seeing, and we use it for looking at things. That's the only technology you need in order to do Visible Work.

Scrum and Kanban boards allow for some of this but they are pretty limited. In the meantime, researchers in the field of education have realised that visible learning is an important element, if not the single most important element, of individual development.[4] More than that, it is possibly the most influential element of how we transfer information successfully between one another or within groups.

Yet most of us have our heads in the screen. We are in doze-mode, anticipating the next big social-platform purchase, the next batch of emails, the next Gotomeeting. What should companies do instead of being victims of the vendor community?

- Encourage people to get their heads out of their PCs, MacBook Airs and other laptops, and talk to each other.

- Provide focal points for really meaningful conversations and interaction (i.e. WALLS). Create conversations, not meetings (put police tape around the meeting room and forbid people from entering the scene of many crimes against humane work).

- Make WALLS so intensely interesting people rub their chins and come up with spookily ingenious ideas they have sat on for months.

We need to create conditions where people empty some of the wisdom that accumulates in their heads out into the flow of conversations that lead to good decisions. It won't happen with Windows or IOS or Android. It needs vocal chords and the nurturing of confidence—characteristics that are not for sale.

To create social interaction you have to make the visualisation of work a key component of change. This idea is core to **flow**, so we'll leave it at that for now.

4

You can read more at John Hattie's site:

https://visible-learning. org/hattie-ranking-influences-effect-sizes-learning-achievement/

HR AS THE KEEPER OF SILOS

Creating a more visual work environment is of vital importance. But to get there we have to start undermining the hold that HR has on work definition.

In enterprises of all sizes, HR departments sustain the dysfunctional systems that slow work and waste effort.

No individual HR person is to blame. It's simply that traditional workflow reflects the hierarchical nature of firms and their perverse incentives. HR defines roles for people at each level of the hierarchy. They have had decades to do this and to ensure their systems are inescapable. They set goals and undertake reviews of people's performances in order to maintain the status quo. HR is also responsible for the heightened individualism that keeps the hierarchy and work process in place, even at tremendous cost in terms of efficiencies. The individual performance review is the castle wall and moat that surrounds every single person in work. (That's why companies like GE have decided to move away from them.[5]) Part of the silo-culture is that those doing the work are distant from those judging performance.

5
http://www.wsj.com/articles/ge-re-engineers-performance-reviews-pay-practices-1465358463

But wait! What if teams rather than individuals create value?

In our experience, a solution to HR dysfunctionalism is to create Job WALLS: let the people executing change decide what work they want to do, within the limits of reason and resources.

Job WALLS are nuanced. An organisation can post jobs but individual people can post job requests signalling what they would like to work on next. HR can define some of the perks but people can ask each other for job swaps and turn their work relationships into a kind of bazaar—a marketplace run for the people, by the people. They can also use the wall to say "thank you" to people for the work they have done and thereby take over the system of appraisal.

Visualising the process of assigning jobs and appreciation for performance is far more powerful than an annual assessment in an HR file. Take note of this before we patent it.

One purpose of **flow** is to push back on traditional HR power and to give employees more control over their destiny.

In reality HR needs to reinvent itself—HR 2.0, if you like. The term itself should suggest an organisational redesign, not one that defends the past with every sinew. And it should shift from endless administration

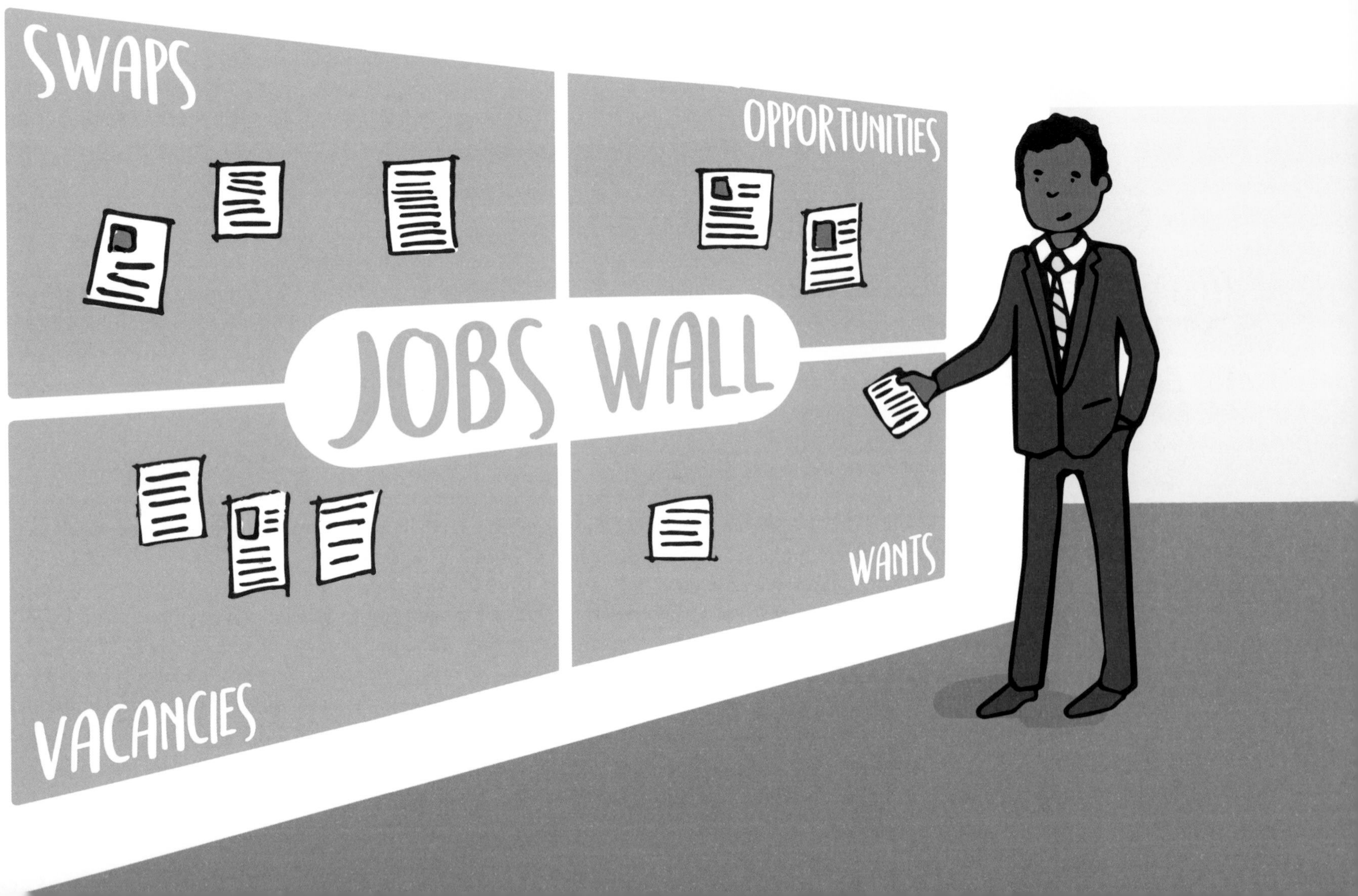
SWAPS
OPPORTUNITIES
JOBS WALL
VACANCIES
WANTS

tasks and being slaves to spreadsheets to taking the lead on topics such as cultural management, mindset coaching, and, dare we say it, **flow.**

Flow can begin in the executive suite, with the Executive Portfolio WALL. It can also kick off with customers and the Customer WALL.

The objective is to visualise and bring collective intelligence to the chaos of information, tools, ideas, and options that surround us as we build new platforms and serve an ever-broadening range of needs. It should be as much a way of work for the CEO as it is for a developer.

But first, it needs to get under the skin of HR, who in turn needs to step out of the way so that opportunity can grow.

Making it work in practice

2. THINKING ABOUT STRUCTURAL CHANGE-MANAGEMENT

Without preempting the rest of the book, we want to give an early insight into how significant change can be managed. The reality that we have just touched upon is that there are too many decisions to be made in too short a timeframe for normal planning structures to be effective. You have to gravitate towards a new system, so how do you begin thinking about that? Where can you begin to frame some guiding principles?

Some baseline principles are:

■ Recognise that the need for speed reduces the power of traditional leadership.

■ Challenge the hierarchy's main rivets and fixing points: role definitions, performance reviews, and individual incentives are all getting in the way.

■ Acknowledge you are already multimodal and have already changed. There are long-term plans (like switching off legacy systems) but there is also the adaptive culture of **flow** to turn planning into a continuous, co-created activity.

■ Hypotheses should be part of the daily routine, the topic of conversations when people meet in the corridor.

■ Decision-making should be a pervasive part of everybody's work and therefore more dependent on the quality of social interaction.

■ The organisation needs a learning model that is almost academy-like, where conversations touch on questions like: What did we learn this week? Who needs to know it? What do we now know that we didn't before? What's next?

What do we mean by multimodal? Most companies that are already several decades old will have at least three cultures:

1 There are the old company traditions and processes that generations of employees get indoctrinated into, including systems like ERPs.

2 There is internet culture, where many processes have become digital and a good proportion of work has gravitated to electronic

What kind of culture are you?

INDUSTRIAL		SERVICE		FLOW	
Production focus	☐	Service focus	☐	Value focus	☐
Siloed IT	☐	Plug and play IT	☐	Cloud, Devops, Microservices, Flow	☐
Technology-led	☐	Design-led	☐	Customer-led	☐
Transactional ERP	☐	Knowledge management	☐	Visualisation and interaction	☐
Closed R&D/Labs	☐	Open innovation	☐	Co-created process model innovation	☐
Hierarchical relationships	☐	Flatter organisations	☐	Business ecosystems, micro outourcing	☐
Protected markets	☐	Globalised, outsourced	☐	Integrated business platforms	☐
Traditional roles	☐	More educated workforce	☐	Creative independent talent	☐
The five year plan	☐	Agile strategy	☐	Continuous strategy	☐
Product push	☐	Marketing pull	☐	Continuous value delivery	☐

More ticks in this column? ☐
Hmm. Let's just call you Adam Smith.

More ticks in this column? ☐
OK - Getting there...

More ticks in this column? ☐
BINGO! You have Flow.

networks. Here, people have adapted Agile methods and there is some interdisciplinary work and large data collection around social media. Very often these have carried rigidity over from Culture 1.

3 Finally, there is the post-internet culture, where the emphasis shifts to real-time decisions and where the priority becomes twofold:

- Aspiring to become far more responsive to customer needs and removing friction from markets.

- Reducing the number of handovers in the organisation (a major source of friction) so that teams begin and complete projects from end to end, roles become more fungible, and processes are shortened.

You will likely be somewhere within these various cultures. In order to think more clearly about it, get together with colleagues and draw up your Culture Wall.

Where do your various activities fall within these three columns?

On our website, we will be providing metrics for you to judge your cultural journey from left to right, from old to modern. For now, chalk your items up somewhere prominently and begin thinking about the journey. You have to convince your people you can make this happen. A map like this lends credibility to the conversations you will have with them.

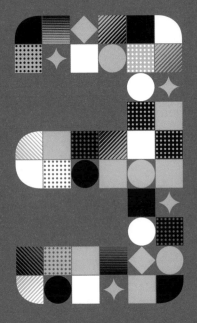

RETHINKIING HOW WE LEARN

JUST AS MOST WORKERS WANT TO CHANGE AND BEHAVE IN WAYS THAT FEEL MORE NATURAL AND ENJOYABLE, COMPANIES HAVE BEEN DEALT A NEW HAND THEY MUST NOW LEARN TO PLAY.

Most organisations are on the cusp of a new future with exciting new tasks to learn and perform. However, when we lack a clear idea of what this consists of most people revert to fearful, primitive emotions about change. That's why the Culture Wall is important— it anchors people's sense of journey.

A fearful mood around change can be especially strong when leaders create negative empowerment or mandate change in ways that set workers up for failure. People who are eager for change then begin to fear it.

Thanks to digital, and new competitive conditions, decades, if not centuries, of Culture 1 are under threat.

And that is exactly the point. The combination of technology, global demographics, connectivity, education, and poor decision-making over time is testing our most traditional beliefs about how value is best created.

Another way of talking about these "traditions" would be "a framework of beliefs". Each and every one of us has a framework of assumptions, beliefs, obligations, and ideas that persuade us to make the trip into work each day. Most of us make that journey having already gone through various change programs.

We are inclined to believe that management is impotent in this important area. The toughest **ask** has become how to make the prospect of transformation credible, and that means engaging with belief. Work wasn't supposed to be about deep convictions and life-shaping emotions but that's where we are at. We are engaged with an emotional maelstrom where employees are vulnerable, ambitious, willing, and fearful at the same time.

All of us make many assumptions that allow us to function properly at work. Sometimes, we go further than assumption and actually suspend disbelief in order to work.

Unless we are strong activists (and Celine Schillinger at Sanofi in France believes we should behave more like activists at work), we accommodate activities we don't like and embrace some that we do. But we are never far away from the pain of contradiction.

We become creative about how to deal with the culture of the company we work for (or we apply to Google), its morality, the condition of the markets it operates in, the likeability of our coworkers, the coherence of the processes or workflows, loyalty to an ideal, and so on.

Taken together these make up the culture of the firm. This reflects a complex framework of checks and balances that we switch on as we walk through the door.

Regardless of your position in the company, that framework is usually what needs to change in today's economic climate.

And whereas people are comfortable changing tools—from, say, a laptop to a smartphone—when asked to engage in changes to their overall framework of belief, people come up against real psychic pain.

Good leaders find a way to allow people to change without threatening their core beliefs. Instead they allow people to adapt within their belief system or grow in ways that are closely related and visibly advantageous and unambiguous.

To do that requires some knowledge of how people learn.

Psychologist Stellan Ohlsson points out that our minds are somewhat bound by past experience and previous frameworks. To explain this, he highlights three stages of learning: getting started, mastery, and optimisation.

Getting started is just that—the earliest stages of learning a task or topic. Mastery comes next, when people have learned enough to impress but not enough to adapt. Finally, optimisation means people are familiar enough with their materials (e.g., knowledge of customers, code, data, etc.) that they can adapt it at will to new conditions.

It's clear that what we all now need is to accelerate our way to optimisation.

Ohlsson's view of learning is that there are also three ways to accumulate new knowledge to the degree that it becomes useful: creativity, learning, and belief conversion. Each of these is important but we want to add a fourth: social interaction, also sometimes referred to as collective intelligence (CI). Most enterprises misinterpret how to apply these learning models.

CREATIVITY

Leaders implore workers to be more creative without really understanding what this means. Ohlsson points out that true creativity is rare because the people who do it well need to devote a lot of time to it.

Implicitly, he argues, creativity comes from hypotheses-testing. It arises when people try ideas out and learn from the various types of feedback they get.

This should not be thought of as a singer belting out a few bars of a new song to see if it sticks with the folks around the piano. We're talking about a long process of imagining new worlds and new ways of thinking and understanding. To arrive at such novelty, creative people will have rejected many, many versions of what they initially thought might work.

Now, clearly there is a parallel with the current vogue for testing out new ideas in business.

One of them is the "fail fast, fail cheap" method, which we've already mentioned. It says we should learn by doing but at low cost. Posit a new feature or function, test it with customers, then bury the idea if it doesn't stack up.

There are two major problems with fail fast, fail cheap. The first, as we said earlier, is that many companies have to make sizable bets and can't rely on rapid-fire shots and continuous experimentation for many important decisions. The second, which Ohlssen points to, is that fail fast, fail cheap doesn't fit the long, painful process of hypotheses testing—refinement, more testing, development, more refinement, and so on—that is integral to creativity. Creative people come to understand how an alternative to the current norms might look but only over time. They work from what Ohlsson calls diagnostic feedback. Here's an example:

Apple began developing a personal digital assistant in the late 1980s. It became known as the Newton. A version of it, the Message Pad, was launched in 1993. The Newton range was abandoned altogether by 1998.

A newer version of the PDA was nonetheless under development in the early 2000s and finally emerged as the iPod. A much larger version of it was ready for market by the mid-2000s. It eventually became the iPad. However, CEO Steve Jobs wanted to launch a new phone first rather than risk further failure with PDAs. He launched the iPhone in 2007, and on the back of that success, launched the iPad 1 (2010), with an eye on a fully featured version iPad 2 a year later.

To realise the iPad 2 and its phenomenal success, Apple began its work 23 years earlier. That is creativity.

Another example would be retiring legacy IT systems. This is a huge task that will involve companies in years of deliberation. Often companies identify legacy as a barrier to change. Another way to see it, though, is as a complex task that requires huge creativity over many years to get right. Seen that way, it has no connotation of failure. It is a truly creative task. Many companies over the past 25 years have abandoned this kind of creativity.

LEARNING TRANSFER

A second way to change is through more direct learning, which means the transfer of ideas and concepts from some other source to us, coupled with the ability to absorb that information enough to re-use it (optimisation).

Most organisations have evolved very specialised and complex rules for how things get done. That's one of the consequences of the large computing systems they adopted in the 1990s. And many of these rules are rigidly enforced.

These ERP systems require people to comply with the rules of an overall system or platform. A slightly more modern example of this would be Salesforce.com, which sets the framework within which sales personnel work.

Learning in this way is similar to learning a language. People may try to do things their own way but in the end they have to comply with rules, even as they run up against the irregularities and illogicality of a language or a system. There is some experimentation (for example, in businesses, Shadow IT) but by and large, employee learning reverts to a norm.

The prevalence of technology platforms has the same effect as grammar. It makes learning rules easier but new ideas become more difficult to generate because of the rigidity that the grammar of technology imposes on what is already a heavily divided form of labour.

The opportunity to change this began from about 2007 onwards, when social media began to take hold. Prior to 2007 most work was organised by a computing system, an enterprise resource planning platform, databases, digital records and so on. Suddenly some elements of work-life gravitated away from fitting in with what the (computer) system demanded of us. Apps, mobile, and social all offered a wider choice of ways to get work done.

The plethora of apps (by 2010 they numbered in the millions) offered choices that made computing enjoyable in a more rudimentary and less structured way. As a result of these consumerised systems, workplace computing switched emphasis away from systems of record to systems of communication and interaction.

In the midst of all this, companies suddenly needed a new "playbook," or guidelines, and a template for becoming more capable of digital work. What became available were more platforms, especially "social business".

There had been an enterprise 2.0 movement in the early 2000s that morphed into social business around 2012. But these new platforms still placed a heavy emphasis on rules-bound work and tasks that were so subdivided that organisations remained full of handover friction.

People had to become activists in order to secure the right to use simpler technology at work, such as smartphones. This was a cause of even more friction but they won! And for the first time in most people's memory they began to break out from an outdated learning system that was very rules' based.

Now we are at a new pivot point: Business needs employees to participate in a system that they must help to define (though the new system is ill defined and poorly understood by many enterprises); and they need to learn how to be productive while they change.

This was once thought to be impossible. In innovation circles most people still argue that you cannot do innovation and execution at the same time. But now we must, even though many people's behaviour is strongly conditioned by the rules-bound past.

This situation causes confusion as we seek to define what that new system should be.

Recently, one of us worked inside a major high-street bank in London, where executives were tasked with making significant changes—lots of them. They hired a consulting company to come in and teach them how to do Agile.

The consulting team's work lasted three months and, according to the executives we spoke with, it was very inspiring. But once the consultants left, it took just three weeks for everything to revert back to more or less its previous state.

As all that new learning got jettisoned, the bank's real problem became clearer. As long as skilled consultants were on hand to coach, inspire, or even railroad, change happened. Take those people away and there was a massive roll back. Employees were essentially being asked to live two lives—the old one with its rules and deference and the new one with its teams and agility (though we question whether Agile truly delivers that).

The key is that there had been very little change

in the way decisions got made or in the relationships in the hierarchy. No new leaders emerged or were even allowed to. Existing leaders continued to spend their time in expensive boardrooms overlooking the City of London, having created the perfect storm of negative empowerment.

Which is all to say that unless leaders change, the many new skills their teams learn will be wasted because staff will always be anticipating yesterday's leadership responses.

BELIEF

As we mentioned earlier, people often find it extremely painful to change their minds on an issue where their views are reinforced by beliefs. Ohlsson's explanation is that we hold different levels of belief in our minds—often contradictory ones.

Imagine it this way: You might, in your private life, be a Christian. But you could be a protestant, Catholic, or Coptic. The core belief is Christianity; the non-core beliefs are these denominations.

Something of these same core versus non-core beliefs exists in science, too. The author Thomas Kuhn outlined this in his book **The Structure of Scientific Revolutions**.

When people have assimilated enough information to support a core belief, they are very reluctant to accept evidence to the contrary.

Re-read that sentence. Even scientists are reluctant to accept **EVIDENCE** that contradicts a core belief. We need these core beliefs so we can build knowledge but because we have core beliefs, we can't change our minds easily.

We hold many beliefs about the workplace. We buy into corporate culture, to a degree. Or some people retain their non-work culture and create friction for others at work. We have beliefs about where work should be based geographically. (That's a key driver of immigration politics.) Very often, we also have beliefs about how the company could do things much better. All of this amounts to a complex framework that is just plain difficult to navigate.

In order to change our minds about these things, we need a new framework or core belief. We need to work imaginatively with people's existing or hidden beliefs.

Often, change is more readily accepted if it can be couched in terms of those existing beliefs.

Here's an example: In the 1980s two doctors, Barry Marshall and Robin Warren, argued that stress did not cause stomach ulcers, bacteria did. This contradicted a core belief in medicine, that nothing survives in the acidic environment of the human stomach.

The theory was rejected outright because the prevailing orthodoxy blamed stomach ulcers on spicy food or stress, not bacteria. Marshall and Warren were not gastroenterologists and the science of the stomach belonged to this latter group.

Now, here is an interesting aside: In the 1930s it was already known that bacteria do indeed live in the stomach. However, by the 1980s the collective consciousness of medicine had more or less forgotten that fact.

After about a decade of argument, Marshall and Warren finally started to get traction with their theory of stomach ulcers. They were ultimately awarded the Nobel Prize for Medicine in 2005.

Acceptance of the theory, though, went through many phases over a very long period of time. One of these was to open up a whole new vista for gastroenterology. In place of a theory that led to bland food for patients, there were now two major new research agendas focused on the role of inflammation in disease and on the influence of the biomeme, the collection of bacteria that exists inside each of us. The gastroenterologist became more important, not less so.

Changing belief, in other words, is inhibited by the knowledge we are committed to. Ohlsson says that change is easier when the next phase of development can be framed in the context of the core belief we are asked to leave behind. Clearly it is also helped by the presence of new oppurtunities.

How does this translate to work life?

Many people will take a skeptical view of the firm they work for. Loyalty or engagement is in short supply, especially these days. However, in order to work successfully, people need to believe that the firm has their interests at heart somewhere along the line. There is also every chance that people will have been through a change-management program at some stage in their work lives and feel grievances about how they were treated during the process.

They may therefore hold several beliefs:

■ The firm won't prioritise me; I am expendable.

■ All work environments are ambiguous but I work for the people alongside me, my friends and colleagues.

■ Top management doesn't see what I see and I

think they are getting it wrong.

- Change programs just don't work.

What is truly important, though, is to identify the person's core belief. It might be none of these. It might be: **Work could be a whole lot more interesting than the company allows it to be**.

Take that on the chin: It could also be, **Change means they will get rid of us**. If that's the case, you will not win people over to a new way of working.

We're assuming you want to change with the people you already have. But we know you will move some people aside in the course of this process.

Before you do that, think about core beliefs:

Change will only take place when it somehow uses the core beliefs that people already treasure.

In our experience, most people believe work could and should be more interesting. If leaders deliver on that, if they make the promise and keep it, then people will work harder and will go the extra mile, ambivalence will slide into the background and the instigators will have won their stripes as effectual leaders. This is perfect startup culture and it begins with a commitment to each other.

Of course not everyone will buy into the promise, and some people are just plain toxic. For the good of the group, you have to move them on.

SOCIAL INTERACTION AS A LEARNING MODEL

In our experience many leaders will avoid accepting the truth about how we learn because they are primed to give orders and expect alignment. Yet a closer look at creativity, learning and belief reveals that each is really about the quality of social interaction.

Learning quality is defined by the interaction between people rather than interaction simply being a pipe through which information is channelled. We acquire all we know from interaction with other people. Even those of us from the school of hard knocks butted up against other people sometime, someplace and came out the better for it. This is quite profound for businesses that need to be hyper-adaptive, because in the past they have often stripped good interaction out of their cultures. Leaders are not skilled in creating the conditions for good social interaction. We, the employees, have learned not to expect it. That's the situation we need to change.

The software sector is perhaps the most advanced learning environment available to us and should serve as an example to the rest of the firm, not to mention society at large, because it embodies this principle.

In the software community, learning is multifaceted; it is offline and online and it is always a peer activity.

Developers are guided by the vibe they pick up in online forums. They interact with peers at meet-ups, engage with open-source software, go to conferences, read white papers, and pick up essential code tricks and workarounds along the way. And they usually give back. They are great at reciprocating and thereby ensuring that the code that supports the systems of most major companies and many smaller ones is really a commons. It is co-created by a vast community and essentially belongs to nobody.

They might need to learn a new language, which they can do on YouTube where various people will have left instructional videos for the benefit of the community. They learn about new infrastructure or architecture designs from their participation in open-source projects. They pick up clues on how to make judgments about good code as they observe the decision processes in communities or in a commit process. Their meet ups or garage events take them outside the firm into the hands of peers. All their learning is an interaction.

This is an example of collective intelligence in operation. It is profound because it shows how important interaction is in accelerating people towards optimising their knowledge.

What is the collective? A sum of interactions. And it shapes and channels vast amounts of possibilities towards practical goals (software design, code,

6
L'intelligence collective: Pour une anthropologie du cyberspace (Collective Intelligence: Mankind's Emerging World in Cyberspace)

applications, business logic, and opportunities). There are now billions of open-source lines of code and hundreds of thousands of open-source projects, not to mention the might of GitHub where information is channeled to good effect. If that is the 'collective' what is the meaning of intelligence in this context?

When applied to collective intelligence it means many things. The idea of CI was originally framed by French philosopher Pierre Levy,[6] although some theorists date it back to the 18th century. In the 20th century, writers like H.G. Wells talked of a "world brain". Democracy, in a sense, could be thought of as a collective wisdom. Economists have tried to describe the stock market as basically a collective intelligence system.

Levy meant something else. In Levy's way of thinking, collective intelligence is not crowdsourcing. It is not about producing a better result or solution through the application of a crowd's many eyes, though this can be a valid activity. It is really about the pervasiveness of knowledge, its ceaseless, abundant flow, and the difficulties we have creating value when there is so much information buzzing around our heads.

He believed that the production, retention, and adaptation of knowledge is a task we are all engaged in—an idea very much tied up with the connectedness of our digital age. For today's firms, that means thinking of knowledge or skill flows as we used to think of cash flows. Knowledge flows in and around all of us, every employee or business owner. And it is far too abundant to master. Collective Intelligence represents the many actions all of us take to make sense of it.

We cannot "manage" knowledge on the scale it is now produced and distributed. We have to learn how to shape the flow in order to produce value.

This changes the fundamental conditions in which learning takes place. It is no longer enough to talk about creativity, learning, and belief. These attributes will not shape knowledge flow.

Social interaction of the type we described above, when referring to software development, shapes knowledge. It makes over-abundant knowledge usable.

There is another aspect of this:

As traditionally conceived, knowledge was something transmitted between people through mechanisms like books, or it went from one to many via a lecture or TV series. But when you begin to view knowledge as a growing and over-abundant external flow, you start to concede that, in the online space, we are all playing a role in shaping it and honing it for use.

In fact, scientists now conceive of the human mind in this extended way.[7] For millennia, science associated the mind with the brain, and the brain only, or argued about a brain-body duality. But more recently, the study of mind has become the study of extensive social influences, and even objects, on the very idea of what makes a brain. The neural patterns of thought are one way of shaping pervasive external stimuli.

None of this invalidates what Ohlsson says. But it should give us a stronger sense of how important good interaction is to a knowledge-driven economy. In this economy what we can know in a way that is useful to very rapidly evolving environments is enabled by how willing people are to communicate and help shape the flow.

7

"The Extended Mind"
Andy Clark & David J.
Chalmers Working
Paper 1998

In Summary

3. PRIORITISING CHANGE

These new ingredients now need to be layered on top of traditional learning processes:

- We shape our minds by how we interact.
- Our interaction helps shape the over-abundant information flowing around us.
- Our experience is of collaboratively managing the flow.

We can only really learn in the flow and increasingly we need to shape knowledge collectively.[8] In the next chapter, we will look at more evidence that good work stems from good social interaction.

There is one interesting addition to this new concept of knowledge and learning. Here again, the concept of **flow** plays a major role. In game design and in literature, there is acute awareness now that to win commitment from gamers or readers there has to be a constant flow of puzzles and solutions.[9]

An engaging workplace operates in exactly the same way. To change the whole system at work, we have to create a flow of problems that people can actually solve.

(In contrast, we often ask them to do the impossible or the trivial.) Good work design is like good literature: it lets people develop an interest and whets the appetite to come back for more.

By the time you have read this far, you will have some new assets to help you think about **flow** in this context:

1 **The Creative Long View:** You will be realistic about creativity and see it as a long-term goal. The core focus of creativity is the very big question of how to migrate big legacy systems, in whatever form they exist. Creativity means taking time, exposing possibilities to debate, trying out a few techniques, and getting feedback. It is the long journey from the left hand side of the column in your Culture Wall to the right. It is exacting.

2 **Getting to Optimisation:** Traditional learning, simply passing on new information, is still an important part of workforce practice. However, it belongs more to the intermediary work activities such as learning how social media works, understanding web skills (software, SEO,

A/B testing). These are all essential learning tasks that have a place in the corporate learning model. They have to be couched in the right context. They are a way of learning where we see the bigger goals of the collective. Getting to optimisation is what many people think of as creativity. However, it is both less than this and more. It is profoundly social.

3 **The Core Belief:** You will have begun to work with people's core beliefs, taking the deep responsibility of ensuring that you, the leader, deliver for them and that they have the opportunity to win confidence and develop new interests. In Chapter 7 we are going to suggest a leadership roadmap for getting you to that point.

4 **Conditioning Social Interaction:** Your role as a leader is to shape the flow. You need to set the right conditions for people's interactions as they help you to frame work division, identify good tools, allocate work tasks, and learn. You will have begun pushing hypotheses

to your colleagues about how to get things done differently. Your first reaction to a new suggestion will be "Interesting! how can we test that idea?" Demand of yourself and anyone else that all speculation about what could be different becomes testable in some way. Identify the next Best Action. People need to be pushed to co-decide what is the next best action for a team or project to take when an idea is up for evaluation.

For example, if we need to create a new customer-centric solution:

- How would that be broken down into chunks of work that each has a clear value?

- How can we establish an experiment or review that provides a proof point?

- How do we describe the customer involvement in the process and how we would engage them with the end goal?

- How would we apply our Go To Market model to this process?

- Given all that, what is our **Next Best Action**?

8

Here is an interesting account of that process:

http://www.strategy-business.com/blog/How-to-Accelerate-Learning-on-Your-Team?gko=28658

9

Peter Turchi A Muse and a Maze: Writing as Puzzle, Mystery, and Magic, 2014, quote by Maria Popova, BrainPickings.com

THE BASIC PRINCIPLES OF *FLOW*

GOOD DECISIONS COME FROM GOOD SOCIAL INTERACTION AT WORK.

The goal of work is to create value for customers. But right now the competitive environment means there are multiple aggressive claims on customer attention. In our view being adaptive enough to compete in this unique environment originates in being social. We get to do things differently when we give each other permission to do so. If we don't give at least implicit permissions to each other, we will react as if a new way of working is anarchic. It will feel out of place and scary. One purpose of good social interaction is to further the needs of learning and decision-making; another is to support the permissioning of change.

The way companies have been run to date, the idea that value stems from good social interaction seems counterintuitive. Companies run on targets, incentives and penalties. But people will create value when their voices are heard and when they are genuinely liberated from dysfunctional systems. People can be given targets and still be social. A slightly more complicated definition of flow takes account of this:

Good decisions, leading to improved value, efficiency and productivity, stem from good social interaction at work.

Change is inherently a social act and successfully changing culture, or adapting to change, is only possible if people interact with a frequency that they typically do not undertake when they have their heads stuck behind computer screens.

People cannot enjoy interacting on social business platforms, which are perfunctory at best. They don't get a kick out of email. There is no frisson with Messenger. They need to experience the emotions of good human contact and shape knowledge flows together.

Here are four logical steps towards getting good decisions from good social interaction:

- Leaders need to set the conditions for good social interaction and it should be face-to-face.

- The focal point of interaction is the visualisation of work.

- That leads to a further point. We need to infuse teams with the ability to break work down so that it can be visualised at a level of granularity where value becomes clear. Work break down is a missing skill and one with very few experts.

- Visualisation is the forum for critique, suggestion, experience sharing, and ideas about how work creates value. It is the venue for good social interaction.

In a recent session with developers in North America, we were surprised to find that in a group of sixty people teams never interacted with one another. The developers we were working with asked for more time together—like once a quarter. This is madness.

Good, swift decision-making is impossible under those conditions but so too is excellence, because:

1 It implies that those of us responsible for any given task are uniquely qualified to know every single thing about it and don't need to interact.

2 It implies personal silos are better than peers at figuring stuff out. Since when?

Leaders have a crucial role here. Fin, for example, has been a CIO and CTO but he doesn't hide away in a private office to get work done. He takes his seat right alongside other developers.

"If I lock myself away," he says, *"I'm not available to give the kind of advice the team needs if we're to make good decisions. The temptation in my role, when you feel you don't know enough, is to go outside the company for advice. That usually means hiring consultants. It's a protection reflex: don't be exposed with a lack of know-how. The minute you do that, though, and lock yourself away with these outsiders, you destroy trust with your teams. They sense you don't trust them to come up with good advice or decisions.*

And they would be right to think that because you are sending them that signal."

On the other hand, when Fin is sitting right in the developer pool, he notes that: *"People who know more than me about a topic can look over my shoulder and tell me where I'm going wrong."*

This is one way that work becomes a process of co-deciding solutions. In co-creation, everyone has an input at some stage in the flow of work.

That might sound like idealistic language but it is actually quite pragmatic. Most organisations and departments are too large, have too many tasks and priorities, and face too much change for any one person to be the conduit. In other words, there can be no leader, at least not in the way we have traditionally understood that role.

So there is a new kind of delegation that goes with **flow**. Everything is visible, transparent, discussed, and decided on the basis of emergent properties, on what we see surfacing in the workflow itself and the interaction between people. Collectively, through good social interaction, decisions get made, plans are fleshed out, poor decisions are spotted early, and good decisions get the support they need.

On top of all that, **flow** lets us discuss the basic values we want to work by.

THE NEW APPROACH TO DIGITAL TRANSFORMATION

Organisations, typically large ones, believe they need big solutions. If they see a problem like a lack of productivity or the frustrations of silos, they expect one big solution to address everything at once - fire people, implement a Six Sigma program, move to holocracy, buy a platform, hire a Big Four firm, etc.

Because we have already laid out our stall—we think change starts with social interaction—we want to say a few words about these big-solution approaches before we promote our own.

From metaphors of war to metaphors of beauty

Ok, there is a hint of provocation here. This book is about **flow** and fluidity. **Flow** is beautiful and very efficient. Water, for example, flows down every hill on the planet and carves out amazing landscapes. That beauty is a reflection of water's hyper-efficiency.

Nothing stops water from finding the easiest route to its ultimate destination.

THE TWELVE-POINT FLOW MANIFESTO

2 Visualise and socialise all work.

Embrace transparency so innovation is not hidden or hoarded. Make it beautiful.

1 Lead by example.

Leaders must demonstrably change. It starts in the C-suite by Walking the Wall and by replacing "that'll never work" with "interesting idea!"

3 Cycle Time is a day.

All work breaks down into a day's work, or less if you can. The smaller the better.

4 Promote the pivot.

Everything is open to change on a daily basis. Being able to pivot is your mantra.

5 Evangelise continuous improvement.

Every day needs to be about finding a way to do things better.

6 Promote the experimental mindset.

Work needs to be about keeping options open. What works today may not tomorrow. The search for new ways of doing things is constant.

7 Define continuous delivery goals through customer value.

The search for, and delivery of, value never stops so all project evaluation is customer centric. Key question? Will my customers share it.

8 Build in emotion.

Walls need to reflect people's desires and ambitions, humour and ingenuity, kindness and gratitude.

9 Build in belief.

Leaders need to accept responsibility for people's beliefs and the dependency that comes with that once they promise a better place to work.

10 Be holistic.

All teams should really be cross disciplinary.

11 Promote continuous learning.

Be purposeful about creating a learning model "in the flow" based on all the social interactions that you stimulate.

12 Co-create all processes.

Even the biggest tasks should get underway without a complete plan and be amenable to changes proposed by people doing the work.

The same applies to work: decisions that get made in **flow** are often automatic, which is about as efficient as it gets. When they are not automatic, they are social, which is a good way to manage complexity.

Traditional business, using the "big" solutions mentioned above, is built upon the heavy application of military metaphors. Traditional work creates divisions, just like armies do. You also take a 30,000-foot view of strategy and target customers with campaigns. This structure is modeled on command-and-control systems.

As individuals who grew up in England in the 1960s and 70s, we recognise these metaphors as somehow normal for the time in which they were created. Back then, the TV was full of army shows of one kind or another, since war-time military structures and culture still permeated our lives. The Vietnam War filled TV screens everywhere and the US and UK were still emerging from the post-World War II mindset.

The problem, as any soldier will tell you, is that armies are extremely inefficient. They tend to plan for the last battle and they are very wasteful. The military metaphor is also downright outdated. It makes it easy to use threatening language around alignment and loyalty but it creates a fearful context for teams.

We know there are far better ideas, metaphors, and parallels for how to work. Let's look at those instead.

Search giant Google recently discovered that there are few productivity boosters as powerfully effective as strong social skills. There's nothing about alignment or order in that idea. In fact, the strongest metaphors we can reach for lie in the language of equality.

In a large study of team effectiveness Google's researchers found that:

"... what distinguished the 'good' teams from the dysfunctional groups was how teammates treated one another. The right norms, in other words, could raise a group's collective intelligence, whereas the wrong norms could hobble a team..."

One reason for the power of egalitarian values is that societal values have changed over the past decade. Norms such as alignment and a certain style of decisiveness that inform command and control are neither effective nor desired.

Google, in its study, found that what works best is a very specific type of respect for social interaction. As long as everyone got a chance to talk, with more or less equal timeshare, the team did well. When conversation was dominated by one person or a small group, "**collective intelligence declined**."

The study also noted that good teams all had "**average social sensitivity**." In other words, they were attuned to the people around them, which underscores the relevance for good interaction.

These results are by no means unique to Google. Social sensibility had been acknowledged as a key factor in boosting collective intelligence long before this particular study.[10]

Being effective is really about the quality of interaction. Good interaction presents its own challenges. It means:

- A new type of leadership that is comfortable with delegating power in a situation where less planning is possible.

- The leader has to spend less time with plans and reports and devote more to emotions and fairness.

- There has to be a commitment to making all work and all decisions visible.

- The ability to invent process, as work is broken down into its logical parts, becomes more important

- Higher levels of personal responsibility are required in teams.

- Comfort with uncertainty is a priority.

- Decisions emerge from interaction rather than from a plan.

We've summarised our views of **flow** in the map above. We took on the word manifesto reluctantly but it is what it is. We think these 12 points are enough to give anyone the full flavour of the philosophy. We aren't calling it a method. It is an approach to the socialisation of work in support of better process design, easier adaptation (pivoting) and more efficient workflow.

In fact **flow** emphasises continuous adaptability. The rigid methods of Agile and Lean do not allow people to continuously adapt processes. They don't help in the invention of new ways of doing work, nor do they necessarily help people to learn.

The new way of work is in fact more experimental than in the past as we chase down the ideas that will become products to defend our market position or promote new business. This experimentation is not fail fast, fail cheap. It is a highly responsible approach to creating options as well as developing the processes that can deliver value continuously. Keeping these 12 points in mind will help create the right conditions for teams to work in the **flow**.

10

Woolley, Anita Williams; Chabris, Christopher F.; Pentland, Alex; Hashmi, Nada; Malone, Thomas W. (2010-10-29). *"Evidence for a Collective Intelligence Factor in the Performance of Human Groups"*. Science. 330(6004): 686–688. doi:10.1126/science.1193147

EXPERIMENTAL CAPITALISM AND THE EXECUTIVE'S BACK POCKET

Experimental work is an integral part of **flow**. It delivers options and it facilitates speed. In essence it gives executives options they can keep in their back pocket ready for the right day to deploy. Experimental environments also need the feedback loops that sustain a creative mindset. In experimental environments hypotheses about risks, opportunities, next steps are all part of routine corridor conversations.

As Janne Jarvinen at the security company F-Secure told us recently, "Much of what we do is no longer on the roadmap. It cannot follow a linear workflow".

In other words, companies have to prepare for the unexpected across a wide variety of their activities, just to be ready for all the different flavours of change coming at them.

This requires what the late author and economist Steven Klepper called "experimental capitalism."

He originally coined the phrase to describe the need for big companies to make extra profits in order to fund the next generation of innovation. We now use the term to describe the need for pervasive hypotheses and testing of ideas.

Many corporate decisions involve big investments.

Very often, these calls cannot be made in the context of a Lean iteration cycle. They require risk-taking in order to get ahead of the game.

A case in point is Jarvinnen's own company. As cyber crime proliferated in and around 2016, F-Secure went out and hired 100 new security experts. They did this on a reasonable hunch that they could build a profitable new business line as cybersecurity concerns intensified. As of the time of writing, they have not had the luxury of developing any iteration cycles to justify the spend on the new hires. Nor have they created a **minimum viable product** to even show that the hires are necessary. They need to go in search of proof points, for sure, to demonstrate the wisdom of the investment and to know how to build out and exploit their new capability. But the investment came good on the day in 2017 when malware shut down thousands of computer systems worldwide.

And that is often the nature of business—companies placing big bets while being somewhat blind to the outcomes.

Sometimes, companies will make those kinds of investments in order to create an experimental environment. All too often, though, they divorce experimentation from the business and call it a "lab". What they really need to do is to nest these investments in existing lines of business as Citrix did with its accelerator program (creating accelerators that invited

The table below summarises where flow stands in relation to other disciplines we've discussed so far in this book.

LEAN STARTUP IN LARGE ORGANISATIONS	AGILE	*FLOW*
■ A structure for product development	■ A structure for software programming	■ *A behavioural context for highly scaled work*
■ Project iteration	■ An *a priori* project-planning method	■ *Engagement process where plans and solutions are co-created and retain fluidity*
■ Risk reduction	■ Risk reduction	■ *Management of uncertainty*
■ Is its own process	■ Fixed process	■ *Continuous process improvement*
■ Cost reduction in successful product development	■ Emphasis on avoiding big failures	■ *Continuous evolution of strategy and capability*
■ No impact on roles	■ More supervisory roles	■ *Fungible roles*
■ Reduces the cost of development	■ Fulfills the plan	■ *Expands options*
■ Innovation method	■ Execution method	■ *A learning model*

startups into the physical building to work alongside staffers). The vogue is to seperate innovation and execution but in future it will be imperative to overturn all of these dated innovation ideas and innovate the process instead.

In either case, you need experimental capitalism, a process that will help you understand the value of everything you are doing with a new investment (as well as existing ones).

You need a learning model so that when you see value, you and everyone around you understands it very quickly. If you fail to develop this learning model, you will lose the value. It doesn't matter if you do Lean, business-model innovation, or Agile, without focusing on value, you are just doing work.

THE FLUID MECHANICS OF FLOW

Flow is an end-to-end system for creating and revealing value through social interaction.

- It begins with the Executive suite, where Executive Walls will help reveal which projects actually have value.

- It incorporates Customer Walls that help identify new market segments and appropriate innovations that provide the triggers for bringing customers in.

- It can include Culture Walls where companies understand their progress.

- It funnels Executive Portfolio Walls into Project Walls and Kanban Walls.

- It might have an Evaluation Wall, where quickfire evaluations take you and the team to the Next Best Action.

- These are supported by Job Walls and Thank You Walls.

- Risks and Issues Walls are also part of the mix.

- These are supported by Job Walls, Cool Walls, Academy and Learning Walls, Customer Feedback Walls, and Thank You Walls.

This is an experimental environment where people can improve the mechanisms for delivering value. The diagram on page 84 shows **flow** as it translates executive priorities into projects that lead (bottom right) to delivery.

Seen from the broader business perspective, there are Walls that feed into the Executive Portfolio Wall, the start point for execution.

As you start working with Walls, the point quickly arises: how do we ensure that the jobs we have in hand are going to create value?

Once a project is in production, once it is going through from Executive Portfolio to Projects in Play to Projects to Team Kanban and then deployment, the question has to be asked continuously.

The same is true if a project is going through a marketing work breakdown process, say from marketing strategy to social-media strategy to individual media-channel tactics. In the case of marketing, data on the effectiveness of tactics is more readily available than it is for a development team. But for both, the question of adding value to the customer experience is an ever-present concern.

By this stage, work is broken down into chunks that allow a low-value piece to be throttled back until more is known or accelerated if it looks good. This capacity for variability is extremely important and a bonus for companies that seek it out.

Nonetheless there is still the question of how to apply a rapid-fire evaluation process. This gets ever more crucial as you grow more aware of the range of new services and products you could and should be offering into the long tail of customers, either directly or via third-party developers. That means an Evaluation Wall.

Projects that need reassessing because of their purpose and value on the Portfolio Wall, or projects that are coming in via a Customer Wall, should be assessed quickly to see if they fit in the development or marketing process.

There's another reason for keeping a separate Evaluation Wall going. Visualisation makes executive interference very public and a matter of record. Very often, in reality, employees hide behind the idea that executive mandates are screwing the company and diverting resources. If it's out in the open then the pressure is on both sides to 'fess up to biases.

Most companies' development teams, innovation labs, or marketing teams become overwhelmed with ideas coming from the C-Suite. Executives drop ideas into the mix without considering how they will affect the team. (And often it is not their own teams that suffer).

Taken together work visualisation on walls changes the nature of the work environment. It not only makes work visible, it also prioritises work issues in everyone's visual field. The walls become venues for interaction, they are adaptive.

There is no right way to do a wall. The only right approach is to encourage interaction. Walls are management tools. They are there for real-time planning. They sustain all 12 principles of **flow**. But essentially, they are there to be designed by you.

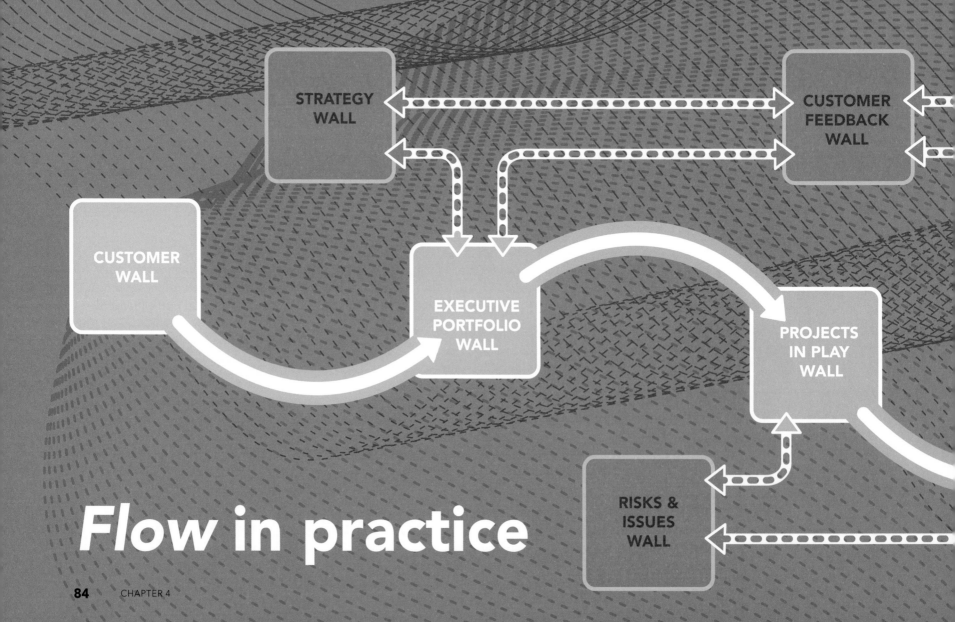

STRATEGY WALL

CUSTOMER FEEDBACK WALL

CUSTOMER WALL

EXECUTIVE PORTFOLIO WALL

PROJECTS IN PLAY WALL

RISKS & ISSUES WALL

Flow in practice

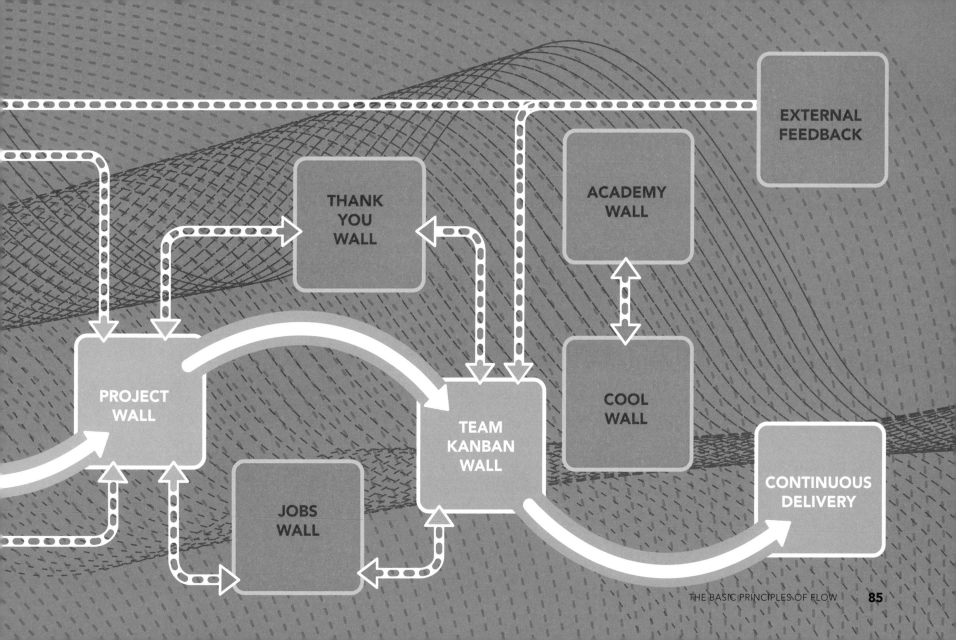

Making it work in practice

4. FLOW FOR PROJECT EVALUATION

We need more and more speed in business. That includes making snap decisions about what to develop. Here are some of our thoughts on how to do good quick evaluations so that people can commit their ingenuity before the big business plan needs writing. Evaluations Walls can have a number of components:

Size. It needs to have a rough estimate of a project's size. We find some great ideas are already half cooked somewhere in the organisation and though they appear big, the pathway to a working prototype can be quick and resource-lite. Use T shirt sizes as in Agile (**S**, **M**, **L**, **XL**).

Value. It needs a known value to the organisation and the customer. The actual business-plan valuation (cash return) is complex and can't be dealt with here. You can have a rough idea of total addressable market but it is far better to ask five things:

1 Which core objectives does the project contribute to? Does it fit a common Go To Market strategy? Some form of Go To Market strategy should be part of the governance of all innovation work. If it doesn't fit with the Go To Market strategy, what are the grounds for treating it as an exception?

2 What is its non-cash contribution? What is to be learned? How will the experience benefit us? For example, is it a project that can be delegated to a local MBA program to help build relationships there? Could it be something to post externally, with a prize attached at a developer Hackathon?

3 Does it have synergy with other projects?

4 Will it help other projects come to fruition faster or will it build learning that can be deployed elsewhere?

5 Which projects might have to give way to it?

With those things in mind, rate the idea with a star system. If you can develop five criteria to judge ideas, rate it out of five; if not, give it a three- or four-star rating system.

Initial Breakdown. What are the top three tasks we should undertake to deliver some value soon?

Horizons. Will it take under three months, three to nine months, nine months or more? With an idea of size and horizon, you can begin to assess how it will impinge on resources.

Action. But now you need to know what to do. What is the Next Best Action for you? Break the project down into its major components by value (say the top three or four things that could create value). What is the Next Best Action to take?

It may be that the Next Best Action is to

- Outsource.
- Wrap the idea into a hackathon day.
- Bring customers in for discussion.
- Offer up a prize to the developer community or a social-media community.
- Work with a specialist innovation-processing site like Innocentive.
- Feed it into an MBA or university science department.
- Drop the project.

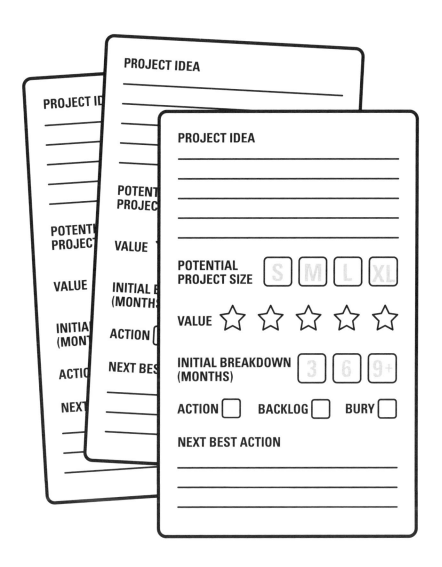

- Just do it.

- Experiment with only a small piece of the idea, assess the market interest, and pivot quickly.

Next Best Actions make you commit to an action, but there is plenty of choice available. That leaves the Go To Market strategy.

The Go To Market Strategy

Having some sense of how and why you might take a new initiative to market is an indispensable discipline in any business. Obvious you might say! But there are important complications that arise when you try to be good about this.

For example, when the car-ride application Uber began to survey the market and design its service, management focused intensely on the upmarket, urban elite that would tolerate its surge pricing model. It was, in effect, a limo service. Facebook did not begin with a global social network designed around mobile. It began as a desktop service for college students in the USA.

Things change, clearly. Pretty soon in the evaluation process, after getting an early idea of value, you need to walk the tightrope. You are trying to find your balance as you consider the relative attributes of value for the customer, service design, achievability and the work processes that will get you as quickly as possible to a good outcome. At the same time you want to maintain flexibility.

Interestingly, the best businesses have a core fluidity that allows them to get to where they didn't know they wanted to be! This strategic fluid core is new yet extremely important. It's the executive mindset we advocate and it's why we talked earlier about the startup potential of large firms.

Thinking like a startup requires a Go To Market model that is not set in stone. Yet, at the same time, it must help to shape the work that you do, day to day and strategically. How you evaluate projects should be guided by a Go To Market model too.

In Lean Innovation the iteration process is all about collecting data. We don't disagree with that but there's more to it.

A good Go To Market model will ask critical questions that help you shape the roadmap of a product or service and help you with the all important work breakdown. Get the work breakdown right and you are halfway to a project plan with pivot points designed into the product or service.

So what will a Go To Market model consist of?

A dozen or more questions that test the value of what you are doing. You can set parameters for these (say score your capability out of 5 on each point) or you can use it to inform the product development process:

1 **What is the total addressable market and is it growing?**

Reason: You are not going to assume you will get a percentage share of this market but you do want to know what's already out there. Ideally your aim is to shift a portion of this market to a new way of thinking and buying through reframing the relationship between price and value.

2 **Is there an underserved market segment of unmet need in your existing markets, or if not does your segmentation imply that you need to shift to new markets?**

Reason: Startups typically spot an unmet need within the existing market of an incumbent. Low cost airlines, for example, created a huge new demand for accommodation and Airbnb spotted a way to meet it before any hotel chain did.

3 **Can the new initiative meet the scale thresholds that your company aspires to or needs before senior executives get behind a new initiative?**

Reason: Your big advantage being in the big Corp is ready-made scale. So, do enough people want to use that new app or will it add to the kudos of existing services that already have scale?

4 **How will a customer discover your new product or service?**

Reason: Define that point in history really carefully. Many companies still think in terms of brute force marketing. Spend some time instead, in the evaluation process, thinking about design attributes that will get attention in a fidgety, low attention, connected world.

5 What might the customer journey be?

Reason: Another essential tool to help with design. Very often a customer journey begins before they come into contact with your product or service and ends after the purchase and use. The customer journey for Tesla cars, for example, begins with poor air quality in cities. The customer journey for photo printing begins with emotion and experiences that people try to capture. Services, in particular, need to embrace this wider reality.

6 How will customers share your product or service?

Reason: Well there are a few reasons why this is critical. Shareability is going to save on the cost of brute force marketing. It will make you more responsive because you need to listen in to what people are saying when they recommend you. And of course recommendation is the dominant form of marketing today.

7 Does the new initiative have synergy across your other product categories?

Reason: Economies of scope. The more you can design in some elements of cross-fertilisation the more effective your spending will be. Amazon.com has an on-demand print subsidiary that helps authors print books that it can sell, as well as Kindle for people who don't want to buy dead trees.

8 What is your traction plan?

Reason: You need to build a strong traction plan if your initial projections fall below the typical threshold that interests senior people. P&G for example wanted new billion dollar businesses. So how will you keep your initiative alive as it struggles to gain acceptance? Who will do the door knocking to get the initiative a hearing with customers? Think about it early on because it may influence design.

9 How big are the achievability issues?

Reason: Technical hurdles that cannot be defined and do not have a work around belong to big companies that invest in R&D-style innovation. That's great but if it is not you then be honest about the barriers to achievability - they can also be cultural!

10 Is there a lead category you will sell into?

Reason: Uber had those urban wealthy folks. Can you define a lead adopter audience you can already begin working with?

11 What is it going to cost and why?

Reason: There are many services where pricing expertise is absolutely critical to a product's success. But today there is a common tiered threshold for online services, say Tier 1: Free; Tier 2 £10 a month: Tier 3 £50. You want to follow the crowd or come up with something more innovative?

12 Will it fit a recurring revenue model?

Reason: More products and services are being offered on subscription because it makes business more predictable and provides cash flow.

There are other questions you might want to embed in a Go To Market model. And not all of our questions will count for you. Like everything else, it is a work-in-progress. But the critical factor is to introduce the model at the outset and let it shape product and service design. The Go To Market model will help define the offering but it will also help you define processes such as where and how to bring in the customer.

HOW TO CATALYSE TRANSFORMATION

LET'S NOW ACCELERATE THE RATE OF TRANSFORMATION.

One of the toughest tasks a leader faces is dealing with the responsibility of being an authority figure that others turn to for help and support. Whether you are the CTO, CIO, team leader, or team member, the idea of others believing in and relying on you is equal parts exhilarating and scary.

At the same time, it is a tough challenge for those needing to learn new ways of work, the employees, to switch their core beliefs. There is a highly charged tango here, with belief governing the tempo and the possibilities of a good outcome.

Leaders need to earn the belief of others while helping them over the psychic hurdles that come with change. Accepting the burden of belief is one of the most difficult responsibilities of leadership.

The surest way to secure belief is to lead the change in a personal way. In this chapter, we are going to discuss that skill.

By taking on the task of self-critique, leaders can show how serious they are about change. Employees who are now completely tuned out at work will come to believe in the company if leaders make promises they actually deliver on. But the promise is hollow if leaders don't take it upon themselves to show the way.

If they do that successfully, a new aura of belief will be focused on the leader and anyone else who puts their hand up for some responsibility. That's the scary bit that leaders often avoid.

Many employees, however, are looking for a leader to unlock something for them in their work lives, like a talent they have had no chance to express, the opportunity to pursue a personal goal, achieve a new kind of work-life balance, or their right to enjoy work.

When leaders unlock these qualities and respond to these needs, work becomes more emotionally fulfilling. Yet the belief this engenders can be a burden. It is a two-sided coin and one side of it we habitually avoid. Leaders have plenty of places to hide from the burden of emotions that belief carries with it. They can act badly because a new strategy demands it (the CFO just pulled budget). They can pull rank or insist on alignment. They may react angrily to missed targets. Underneath all that they can just be scared of what it means to be responsible for the careers and happiness of other people.

There is also a truism that you have grown up learning the know-how of your particular specialism. Maybe as a techie, for example, you started out coding and now know architecture and other related work. That knowledge is part of your career progression and you value it. However, it doesn't make you any kind of leader even though leadership is where you will end up.

It is abundantly clear from studies of high-performance sports that people who play well aren't necessarily great managers. Football players have to earn coaching badges before they get a shot at management. Often they learn more by managing in the lower leagues before they go to the big stage. Leadership is thus a profession in its own right.

There's an appropriate parallel here with graduating from a role that's all about function, like technology architecture or product management, to leading changes in the way a team performs. Specialisms don't fit people out for that leadership.

Again, let's emphasise we are not advocating creating

a touchy-feely workplace. Speaking pragmatically, though, the role of leaders has changed. To deal with today's demands leaders need more emotional, non-functional, skills than ever.

Dealing with belief is far and away the most difficult emotion for the leader to deal with, especially for the one whose job is on the line.

People who believe in you go home happy. In turn, they make good decisions for you. But to maintain belief you have to be consistently open, able to lead by example, be ready to delegate, and be attuned to people's broader needs. You must avoid command and control and learn to live with the responsibility for how other people feel.

There is a shorthand for this panoply of leadership assets: you need to accept the emotional burden of leadership.

The way to get started down that road is to face up to the contradictions that get suppressed at the highest levels of the leadership group.

Most companies have a culture of leadership that separates them from employees, and not just in terms of salaries (where there is often a huge gap). The really painful gap lies in what leaders expect of employees and what they are prepared to subject themselves to.

This is particularly stark in the field of innovation and transformation where, as we have already stated, leaders mandate change and then go back to the sherry cabinet or the hospitality lounge at a sports ground and carry on as normal. This hypocrisy is sometimes compounded by visibly bad decision-making. Many employees have a sense of the wrong decisions that leaders take and are forced to let it happen.

A concept we refer to as **Walking the Wall** can change that. It is a highly visible wake-up for senior management that exposes decisions to peer scrutiny. In turn, it will save resources and bring a new sanity to employee relations. It takes a true leader to execute on it because it halts the pretence and half truths that enterprises routinely generate. In place of those, it instils belief.

Whether the executive suite likes it or not, we are inevitably moving towards a real-time context for decisions both large and small.

High-growth startup Skyscanner's innovation rate (mentioned earlier) is setting a new standard but there are other companies with extraordinary velocity ambitions. Amazon.com already deploys new code every 11 seconds and craft selling site Easy commits 50 major deployments every day. While figures this high seem remarkable now, they will soon become the norm for many companies

All leaders have to grasp this salient fact—that hundreds of adaptations per day will be commonplace soon.

Getting to that degree of efficiency, and automation, involves:

- Growth through real-time innovation.

- Managing huge uncertainty about what may or may not work in innovation environments.

- Creating an experimental context at work to give employees the best chance of success (through testing, permission to do new things, delegating choices about where to make changes, and so on).

- Recruiting and developing the best people possible.

- Building trust with and between them.

- Transparency in information.

- Acknowledging that no single person can make all this happen.

That last point is perhaps the one that needs to guide modern leadership philosophy. It is not saying "no single person can run a company". That much is obvious.

It means no single person, no source of authority, can truly oversee all the change that needs to happen today at work. Even "business as usual" involves too high a degree of change for "management as usual". It means the leader's role and identity, especially at the very top, has to change.

The point of entry for change-management therefore is the culture of leadership. That's a tough challenge. Huge egos are at stake. But leadership has to evolve from "I lead the way that this company executes its business" to "I lead the way this company changes itself each and every day."

Now we come to the first practical steps: You need to walk the talk.

We realise many people reading this will not be members of the C-Suite but bear with us. You can learn a little of the radical and quirky activity that we draw leadership teams into or you can skip to the next chapter where the leadership lessons are more broadly based. We think you will enjoy staying with us though.

Leaders need to lead the process of change by example but how do we make sure that is not just an empty phase?

We'll talk you through four practical steps. Our aim with these is to put executive management on a different and better footing, one where they demonstrate their willingness to change and in the process yield very tangible results quickly. We call this technique **Walking the Wall**. Here are the steps:

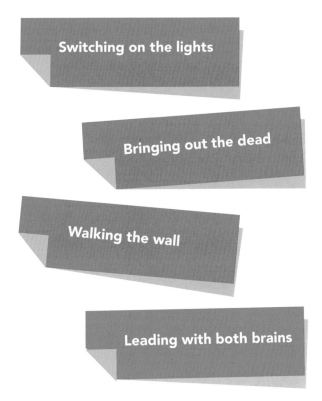

Switching on the lights

Bringing out the dead

Walking the wall

Leading with both brains

Switching on the Lights

Executive suites are a great place to start a revolution because there is so much space: wide corridors, long walls, and fewer doors breaking up the wall spans.

It is quite the norm for the CEO or head of HR or Facilities to festoon the corridor walls with modern art or, worse, antique paintings of horses.

This is exactly the place to start the leadership of transformation and only a fool of a CEO would object. Take the paintings down and turn the wall into a whiteboard. This will be your first Executive Portfolio Wall and you need the space to put up project cards.

Ok, so in sequence:

1 Before taking down the (horse) pictures arrange for the company's portfolio managers to draw up one card for every project under their purview. Not just every product, but every project.

2 Make sure they include projects that are in blacklog—that is, the ones not yet started and those that are in the early stages of formation.

3 Mark each card with a t-shirt size: small (S), medium (M), large (L), and extra large (XL). These will reflect, roughly, the spend on the project. But keep it simple at this stage.

4 Now take down the paintings and create the whiteboard.

5 Create one column per strategic corporate objective. There should only be five or six of these.

6 Pin the cards under the strategic objective they are meant to help deliver on.

7 Add a picture of a customer to each card, if the project directly benefits them.

8 Lastly, add the value, preferably in monetary terms, of each project.

9 Where cards do not fit neatly into a strategic-objective category, place them under **OTHER.**

You now have what's probably the first example of your company visualising all of its project-resource allocation. This information is usually hidden away in spreadsheets, project reports, and personnel evaluations. But here it is, at long last, out on view with the light shining on everything you are doing as a company (or division, or unit).

Before you bring out the dead, just let the CEO, CMO, CTO, or whomever else sits up there in the C-Suite get a taste of the scale of what's going on in the company.

Over time, they will get to see progress on the Wall (such as projects reaching their objectives) but the first blush of the sheer quantity of tasks happening, the sheer burden their people are working under, will open their eyes. It always does. And there will most likely be a second immediate benefit. At least 30 percent of projects will visibly have no place among the strategic objectives of the company. They are zombies or they are superfluous. Or maybe they are signs that the company is intuitively reaching for new goals!

Bringing out the Dead

We have begun to see which of the projects have real value and how well they fit with corporate objectives. Executives usually create these objectives on their annual off-sites, and the list doesn't vary much from company to company. It tends to go something like:

- Customer front and centre.

- Going digital.

- Offence: delivering upside through new market entry; increased share of wallet.

- Defence: cost focus/rationalisation.

- Prioritising innovation.

For the most part, these priorities emerge from very sparse information. The company that has senior executives able and willing to pore over vast tracts of data and insight to set more detailed objectives is rare. Instead, C-Suite tend to work with the summaries that managers produce.

Haydn explains a little further:

"Recently, I had to produce a plan for a potential new platform-based service for a major bank and created significant data to justify it. Of course, it ran to about thirty four powerpoint slides, which I thought was brief. The pushback was incredible: I was told to get it onto 3 slides, maximum. That wasn't even for C-Suite executives. We were working two levels below that but the explanation I got was, 'People at this level don't read. They probably won't go past the first slide'".

Visualisation helps people get over this "Won't Read" self-importance.

When you draw the company priorities on the Wall and categorise all the project cards under each priority, what usually happens is that you see a heap of leftover zombie projects. These were usually created in a rush to please executives after previous strategy sessions or off-sites, where senior employees gathered together to respond to the latest management fad or the needs of a new appointee. They are pet projects that an outgoing executive did not kill or that the CEO won't admit are a waste of time.

In fairness, some of them may be projects that a brave executive has launched in the hope of pushing a new strategic agenda. That's great. To reveal it is to give it life.

Whichever way the Wall goes, executives need to face the harsh winds of peer pressure. It will help them unwind expensive and useless projects and provide focus for those that are left. The Executive Portfolio Wall helps because it brings folly and wisdom into the open.

What you are aiming for is to understand what the stack of cards under OTHER really means. In our experience a ruthless evaluation will produce many of them. Try to categorise some of these into what we might call a hidden priority—a set of tasks or projects no one has front of mind but is nonetheless active and resourced.

What you have at this stage is a record of projects that

are contributing nothing or at best little and a record of emerging priorities.

You will also find that one or more of the priority categories is actually very lightly resourced, and one or more objective will be sucking in XL T-shirts like crazy. But now you can see it.

Walking the Wall

It's time now to interact with senior colleagues. Take them out of the boardroom and corner office and Walk the Wall with them. Invariably the reaction is going to be: OMG, so many projects!

Yes, so many projects.

As you Walk the Wall, you can go into any degree of specificity on what it shows. But the best route to take is usually to let senior people discover for themselves just how skewed resources really are. Where you are leading them to, at a high level, is:

- Finding No. 1: There are a lot of zombie projects.

- Finding No. 2: The company is not prioritising the projects that have real value, even if people think they are.

- Finding No. 3: There is an imbalance in resource allocation.

- Finding No. 4: The company has created ways to block its own progress by not being rational enough and that, more than anything, kills the goodwill of your best people.

To be less flippant for a second, the tasks described above are not easy to accomplish. The CEO does not like to see his or her living space taken over by other people. The walls were fine the way they were. It is not easy to convince important people that they should be more enlightened about their company.

But now the total work volume has been visualised in a way that the CEO and her colleagues can interact over. It has created a picture that team leaders from across the company can consult and interact around.

Chances are they will all be surprised and they will have no idea, really, what the company's resources were actually being spent on. Sad but true. They will have overlooked many of the pet projects that are still eating up time and money.

The reason for this is people at the top set priorities and leave the executing to others. At best the execution teams refer back to those priorities for a project "green light". At worst, they struggle on, trying to get resources for stuff that has already become irrelevant. Chances are, too, that senior leadership has never confronted its own complacency before.

By exposing all this, new conversations can begin.

Leading with both brains

What you have just accomplished is switching executive thinking over to what really matters.

Here's Fin's experience:

"In one of my roles, the portfolio managers helped me create a wall that showed a total of 380 projects underway in the company. That's actually not a huge number but the company was turning over only around $3 billion. The project volume was enough to shock everyone in the management team. Being in silos, they'd never seen it all at once before.

Just as important, though, a high proportion of those projects either did not match priorities or were legacy.

The CEO was making the familiar pleas for the company to change its culture, particularly its IT structures, so that they could be more nimble. We were about to hire a consulting company to help us. And while we went ahead with it for a few elements, we did

so much further down the line. Had we followed the initial urge to get the experts in early, the resources to pay for them and their plans would have been hauled out of someone's budget in a routinely aggressive way, like making everyone find a way to save 5 percent on their spend that quarter.

What I wanted to do with the Wall was show the CEO several features of the company as it existed there and then, because very little in a change-management process would affect this. Typically you "change-manage" without bothering to be honest about what's wasted in the company. And change-management tends to come on top of what's already there. It becomes one more project that just sucks an equitable spread of money out of everybody's budget.

It was clear we were under-resourcing change, even though it was a priority. In that part of the Wall, we were committing too much to legacy IT when a cheaper and better solution existed in the cloud.

We were misallocating a lot of other resources, too, over-prioritising projects in areas of the business that had strong managers who were simply better at getting the green light.

A third insight was that several of the projects these executives had given the green light to were still in the backlog. Resources had been eaten up by projects of lower priority. New projects could not get underway.

We discovered that if we could get rid of the bad projects quickly many of the resources could go towards the changes that were actually needed. Being nimble does involve a lot of process change, but it also involves getting rid of the dead projects that are a weight on the company.

I see five insights from Walking the Wall:

1 Knowing how much you are actually doing and the pressure that puts on people.

2 Knowing that a sizeable share of that work is wasted. You can't turn away from waste when it's there in front of you, six feet high. Here are resources you badly need and they are there being squandered in zombieland.

3 Knowing where priorities are skewed and need quick realignment.

4 Knowing something about the hidden priorities that we didn't know we had. Are they good or bad?

5 Knowing that you have created policies and processes that needlessly get in the way of efficiency, block any attempt at doing change

better, and frustrate the life out of talented staff. There they are right in front of everyone's eyes. You can't duck them.

If you don't find a way to fess up to this stuff, you are managing the business on behalf of the C-Suite's sensitive feelings, which is nonsense. Visualising all this brings out the opportunity for a more creative form of management that's enjoyably rigorous."

We call this leading with both brains because generally today the plea goes out to think in more creative ways. But real creativity, as we said earlier, arises in the context of big decisions and big transformation. Switching on the Lights, Walking the Wall, and Bringing out the Dead are the beginning of a more creative leadership team capable of guiding solutions to the problem of transformation.

The Executive Portfolio becomes a permanent tool for strategy and portfolio management. Over time (see page 105) you add more and more information to it. It becomes a reference point for everything that executives do and is incredibly useful for people responsible for project execution.

Making it work in practice

5. STARTING THE FLOW

Changing the big picture at the highest levels of leadership is the only way real transformation will happen. Let's assume you have that opportunity. What comes next?

The portfolio managers have to go away and produce real estimates of project cost and value. Meanwhile you can enrich the Wall with more visual information.

As the portfolio managers do their job and provide the data, executives will start to rip down cards that are so obviously resource wasters. Very often they will do this after hours or after a drink or two. But they will also start to think and socialise their insights in the daytime with a degree of energy that no off-site or consulting report would ever provoke.

In place of minuted board meetings, they will stretch their legs between phone calls and take a look at the wall. Bumping into each other on the way to the washroom, they will say things like, "However did such and such a project get the green light?" "Can't believe we wasted money on it for so long!"

A new portfolio will begin to take shape. Team leaders from across the business can copy the cards that matter most to them and take them to their own work area. By now, they will have a Project Wall and can pin those cards up.

This is the start of **flow**. You have begun to create belief because leaders have Walked the Wall and begun the change. A new way to manage is becoming visible (and visualised).

Executives can meet at the wall to review progress or take action. For example, they can reallocate resources to higher priority work or authorise hiring more people. Also if a project is not realising benefits, it is killed and moved to the lower section of the wall as a visual reminder of failed projects. You can of course add other visualisations to rally the culture of continuous improvement.

You should certainly have a project cost and project value on each card but, keeping it simple, visualise these with signs like $, $$, $$$ to indicate the financial importance of the project. Too much detail will create the wrong debate You can have a tweet length description - we find teams love to keep within 140 characters. It's a great discipline. Signal the potential blockers so everyone is alert to risk. Indicate the beneficiaries of the projects and include a target date.

This is now a very rich source of information for everybody to observe and share! But you may want to add more. Walls are freeform. You create them the way you want to.

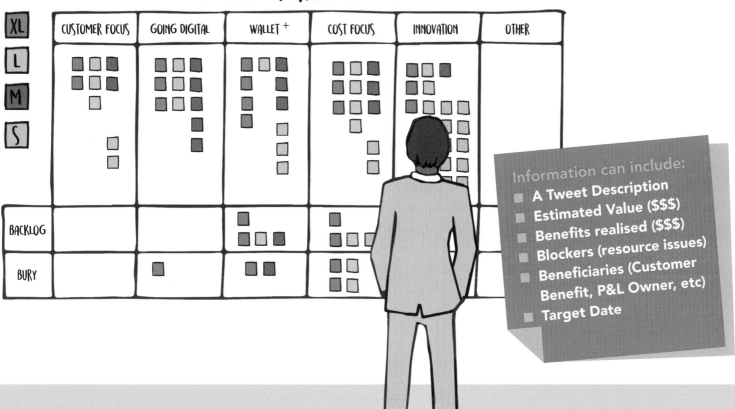

EXECUTIVE PORTFOLIO WALL

	CUSTOMER FOCUS	GOING DIGITAL	WALLET +	COST FOCUS	INNOVATION	OTHER
XL L M S						
BACKLOG						
BURY						

Information can include:
- A Tweet Description
- Estimated Value ($$$)
- Benefits realised ($$$)
- Blockers (resource issues)
- Beneficiaries (Customer Benefit, P&L Owner, etc)
- Target Date

ROLLING OUT
VISIBLE WORK

IN THIS CHAPTER WE WILL OUTLINE A SOCIAL LEARNING MODEL REALISED THROUGH EXTREME *VISUALISATION*.

Visualisations are a method for surrounding ourselves with information about what's happening in the business and how we can contribute our special skills. But more than that they are the focal point for how to do work differently. They are the true medium for change. They allow collective intelligence to happen.

The more you visualise, the more people will learn simply as a product of their interaction around the business of the day. New information will become a built-in part of their visual and social landscape. The walls of the building will become a set of venues where the internal "crowd" can deploy its collective intelligence to shape success. Their work will be much more fully informed and they will have a setting in which to provide the kind of feedback real creativity demands.

Flow, as we've discussed in earlier chapters, is not just a methodology that gets applied to tasks and workflows. It is the toolbox for promoting the interactions that change how your business delivers value.

VISUALISATION AND DECISION-MAKING

People in a **flow** culture are able to accept that many of the decisions guiding their work could change at any moment. They get excited by the presence of uncertainty, primarily because they are co-decision makers. They have agency in the process rather than anxiety about information that is cloudy or responsibilities that are vague.

Accepting what we said earlier about the need to make more decisions, these can be made in the **flow**.

Decisions about features and products emerge from the social interaction of the people doing the work.

At any time, all projects, tasks, and works in progress are visible and tie back to strategic requirements of the firm and forward to the point of delivery. That makes it far more interesting to get up in the morning and make the commute. People can see, literally, the whole picture.

Flow trains intelligent eyes on important tasks and enables real-time decision-making on issues such as the relevance of a work task, its value, the workarounds or tools available to complete it, and so on.

In one respect, executive teams already use visualisation, though they don't realise it's entirely the wrong sort. In fact, visualisation is the most important reflection of complacency in the executive suite or the foyers of large organisations.

Normally the imagery falls into two camps. One will be of the company documenting its achievements, history, and dignitaries through plaques and founder photos. Some companies spend substantial sums of money maintaining these visuals, almost like old obelisks or graveyards with elaborate headstones and architectural tombs telling you about every member of the family.

Our message to you is that this imagery can be significant but it needs to have today's work more clearly embedded or you are creating a museum.

The other camp uses art purchases. Tens of thousands (or even millions) of dollars worth of major artists' work run along the walls of the executive suite and the atrium. The company and executives might also be benefactors of city art shows and museums. There is certainly nothing wrong with supporting artists. We applaud it. But multi-million-dollar pieces of art in the hallway can be interpreted as conceit by the people you are asking to be more creative for you in each of your departments. The message you send is, "We (the C-Suite) have made it! Please keep us in a style we're accustomed to". That is a very provocative message to people whose dedication and commitment you need.

The kind of visualisation we are promoting has nothing to do with the success of the firm yesterday or the self-aggrandisement of leaders today. **Flow** creates a visual landscape from the company's projects and employee roles. We suggested earlier that employees should own the walls, especially Job Walls, Appreciation Walls, and Learning Walls (we will also talk about Cool Walls).

By visualising projects, tasks, roles, tools, and strategy, and by opening them to scrutiny, you increase the chances of success. That starts with the likelihood that you'll be able to dispense with as much as 30 percent of current works in progress and free resources to bring in great new people to do more relevant work.

In essence, you are keeping many critical eyes trained on the company's activities, from top-level decisions down, all with a view to improving them day after day by drawing on the incredible power of many people shaping the flow of information.

People don't need to know every detail of how one hundred projects connect. But if they don't see their part in the mosaic, they will very likely make poor judgments.

A major benefit of visualisation is to keep both the overview and the small details in front of talented people who have access to so much additional information. In turn, they get to play a bigger role and the organisation gets the benefit of their wisdom so that, in Levy's terms, they can help shape the collective intelligence of the firm into ways to deliver better value.

Leadership roles have to pivot to refocus on scene setting, direction, integration, and sense making. To support real-time work and decision-making, leaders need to keep tuning up the learning model. The arrival of leadership as a shaping, nurturing activity reflects the emergence of the extreme visibility principle. As much as can be made visible should be. Here are some examples:

The Customer Wall

The reasons for keeping those real representations of customers we brought up in Chapter One are not idealistic. Realising value is a complex human process and has many gradients to it. When Google, for example, launched its Google Glass project, it looked as though wearables were about to go big.

What happened?

Apart from the immense publicity Google acquired from it, the Google Glass project fell apart because there was effectively no market for Google's version of wearables. Despite Google boasting that its decisions are "based on the data" and that too few companies have as much access to data as Google, the company found no market for what it had developed iteratively with the developer community. (Would it have gained more traction if it had gone to a wider customer base?).

Niche suppliers of heads-up displays (HUDs), such as Epson (HUDs for work) and Recon (ski goggles), capitalised on a growing and tangible interest in wearables but these were intrinsically customer-centric projects (such as how to give skiers more information). Virtual reality got a boost, too (it's an area Facebook bought into). Snapchat is heavily promoting its own Spectacles video camera.

The point is that value comes in surprising ways.

What customers will latch onto and come back for can be extraordinarily unpredictable. What chance do you stand, really, if your walls are covered in art or your projects are solely focused on code?

You need the face of the customer in front of you because you are second guessing, to some degree, what these good people will want. How will having their actual faces, tweets, or other messages allow for this kind of knowledge? Normally, it is a visual cue that triggers our brains to consider what those people might want.

The additional benefit of the Customer Wall, we use Customer Insight walls, Customer Segmentation Walls and Customer Issue Walls, is it focuses developer and marketer interest on the many new segments we can now identify thanks to better data. Today's businesses are driven by scale and scope, the latter representing a substantial broadening of the products we have to offer to a long tail of customers in a cost-effective way. These segments need to be on display and a focal point for a debate. Are the segments an accurate reflection of customer interests? Could we segment more and provoke more thinking about value? If you are not asking these questions you do not have a startup mentality. You are vunerable to disruption.

The Executive Portfolio Wall

The Executive Portfolio Wall is leadership by example. As we discussed earlier, the primary purpose of it is to review how closely works in progress support corporate objectives.

There are times when the fit between objectives and projects is good but there will always be projects that serve no real goal, ones that need to be buried and those that are uncategorised and therefore suggest that a shadow agenda is alive and kicking.

We emphasised earlier that executives typically send bad messages with their visualisations: vintage artwork or modern, expensive art that is a statement of one thing only, that the executives have arrived.

The executive suite has to become a place where the walls are full of work and reflect executive engagement with the businesses they run.

In the course of drawing up the Executive Portfolio—or, more accurately, redrawing it—the Wall should reflect projects that deserve to be live. There will be several of those that are new. They will be migrated from ideas to active status. The feasibility or market analysis will be over and they now have a green light. These go to the Project Wall. The **flow** has begun.

Of course, you may get push back on the whole idea of an Executive Portfolio Wall. You may touch on sensitivities that threaten your confidence or even your career. At the very least bring up the idea of Visualisation, if not physically in the C-Suite, then for starters at an off-site. If you continue to get pushback on the idea of exposing and reviewing projects, chances are transformation is not going to work.

The Project Wall

The Project Wall is the place where work is broken down into components that can be handed over to teams who will then break those down into tasks. In reality, there are two parallel Project Walls: one where project dependencies are visualised and one for initial work breakdown.

The latter is really a place to understand a project in as much detail as can be imagined by experts who ponder the technical and business value and the process implications of the work.

To get a sense of the Project Wall, take as an example the use of drones to inspect car damage, providing insurers with an independent verification of the likely cost of repair.

Few people have worked with drones, which means this, like so many other projects, has a large element of the unknown about it. But many of us have worked with wireless communications and we all have a background in some form of GANNT-like planning. This new project, then, can be broken down as follows:

Project Wall Breakdown

The goal is to explore the use of drones. The first task is to break work down into components that will deliver value quickly, such as:

1 Mapping out a novel conceptual prototype.

2 Sourcing information on drone applications elsewhere.

3 Seeking an opportunity to talk publicly about the concept to secure reputational advantage.

4 Designing a communications plan for people to share the novel concept.

5 Defining and securing (paid) customer proofs of concept.

6 Positing the concept in a base station environment: requirements re: size, location, recharging facilities (self design or bought in).

7 Mapping out control principles for sending and receiving drones, message protocols, security design, drone size and durability.

8 Designing protocols for interaction with people at the scene of an accident (and avoidance), operator sequences and interfaces, and so on.

Many of these facets will go through a feasibility study on the Executive Portfolio Wall. Once they come to the Project Wall, the job is to specify detail. The technical detail will then go to the Team Kanban Wall, while the business detail goes to the analysts or marketer who will have an eye on the Go To Market plan.

The Team Kanban Wall.

Around any office doing good Agile, there are hundreds of Post-it notes related to projects and the different tasks in progress. Anyone can see them. That of course is good Kanban, and it's a sufficient starting point for getting people out of their own personal silos and into the flow of interaction that good work demands.

Team Kanban Walls are perhaps the most important focal point for discussing work allocation, the value of each task and the tools that are going to deliver value quickly.

Teams use this Wall on a daily basis. It facilitates a ritual, a daily stand-up where insights are shared, problems and issues raised, decisions are made, work is allocated, and blockers are unblocked.

The company needs employees to function actively around the Wall not just take a task off and go to code.

- Talk about progress and how to fix blockages or move onto other priorities.

- Tell the product owner or tech lead that the work division looks skewed or some solution is suboptimal.

- Point out that the creation of a new microservice, open-source solution, or tool could lead to a better outcome.

- Demonstrate that a small program or API (Application Program Interface) could reduce the code base and make life easier because the flow hits less friction.

- Illustrate a new solution from a past experience.

- Pull in the next piece of work from the backlog when a team member is free to work on it.

These interventions are how giants of the Internet age like Alibaba prosper.

Very often, projects will hit levels of complexity that need smoothing out, so somewhere in the **flow** a manager might make the decision to push a problem into open source in order to get even more eyes on it. They may commission complexity reduction internally, or use external developers, a University project, or a hackathon or jam.

Risk and Issues Wall

Here, any member from any team can raise risks and issues that teams need to address, everything from a delay in acquiring new servers to concerns about a process or a lack of resources. The leaders, in turn, must either address the risks or accept them for what they are and take their chances. You may not always be able to fix everything but here is a chance for leaders to respond publicly to risk.

This is also a chance to bring up issues with your team. Is it short of resources because the CMO keeps pulling people away? Show you can stand up for your team. Bring the CMO in to explain herself. That, too, boosts confidence.

Fun Walls

Not all extreme visualisation needs to be process based. *"Look across our office,"* says Fin, *"and you will see a Jobs Wall (as described in Chapter 2). It is a space announcing vacant situations in the company but it's more, too. Employees can come here and request a job, note what they would like to work on next, and post their ambitions or where they want to go next. It is a social interaction space for the most important components of our success: the people who work for us.*

There is also a Thank You Wall. It's important that people's appreciation is just as visible as their tasks. If folks want to say 'thank you' to colleagues they can post it here. In that way, people know that they are appreciated, and others can see that appreciation.

I'm currently working on a concept called the Cool Wall (inspired by the TV show Top Gear), whereby team members can post things they feel are really cool and that we, as a company, should investigate. In IT, that could mean new development environments, such as containers, scalable programming languages, or DevOps. In marketing, it might be new social tools, new techniques to scale a Facebook campaign, or a metric that shows the relative losses and gains in traction between Pinterest and Instagram.

Programmers play with this stuff in their spare time long before it hits corporate consciousness. It's what they do in their open-source communities or pick up from mates in startups. Marketers should be equally interested in the tools of their trade and feel a sense of reward in sharing that.

A Cool Wall will celebrate innovation and creativity and bring it out from shadow activities in order to make it real. However, the other end of the wall (not so cool) may actually contain many of our existing assets, stuff we've built or started and isn't appropriate any longer but that no-one has had the time, gumption, or insight to kill off. I'm thinking about that as a point of comparison. I'm not too sure if it will create negativity. But we'll try it and see."

The Digital Business Wall

There used to be a division between marketing and IT. In many cases, there still is but it has to be bridged. The Digital Business Wall is one way to do that. Most marketing functions are increasingly dependent on some form of technology and therefore some form of software development.

In recognition of that, you now see the great consumer goods organisations of the world (Unilever, P&G) trying to figure out ways of creating a technical ecosystem where marketers and IT people interact on equal terms. In the old days, a company could hire an ad or marketing agency to do its work but today you are lost unless you are familiarising yourself with AI, chat bots, automated customer service and social-media analysis, and automation. These are essential technical tasks that marketers bring their own unique cultural insights to.

Unilever has pioneered The Foundry as a way of creating an ecosystem of tech companies that can help with these innovations. Tech companies can propose any number of solutions to The Foundry, which acts as an innovation hub for Unilever's business lines. Think of it as a hub-and-spoke model with innovation coming into the hub from aspiring tech companies and going out to the business lines.

There is only one problem with this model: it needs a point of integration. It needs a visualisation where the whole potential of the tech community is visible as part of a process. What might the new Unilever marketing process look like?

That's an important question, and the answer will be continuously unfolding. If that answer is left in a spreadsheet or report, it will not be understood by enough people. It has to be equally visible to the internal IT shop, which will invariably have a role in integrating new solutions.

Earlier we talked about the Customer Wall. The Customer Wall allows companies to visualise new market segmentations. A similar segmentation can be constructed for new technical solutions. The start point can be the Customer Wall: Given these new customer needs, what are the technical solutions? Or it can begin with the question: Given the inevitability of AI in the consumer-facing organisation, what processes will be most affected?

Other questions might include: Where do we have to rethink our approach to marketing? What will the new steps look like? The task of identifying these new steps belong both to marketing and IT.

The Digital Business Wall is a different view of the change process. The IT shop is primarily focused on what comes off the Executive Portfolio into the Project Wall. Marketers and business analytics have a role in defining the breakdown of a project at that point. But marketers and IT have to take a view of transformation as a whole, and negotiate what digital processes mean for how employees work together.

Obeya

Of his Obeya wall, Fin says, *"My ultimate dream was to have a room where I could visualise all the critical projects in progress and provide a white space for ideation,*

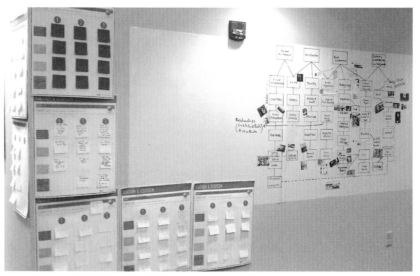

This page and opposite:
Walls at work

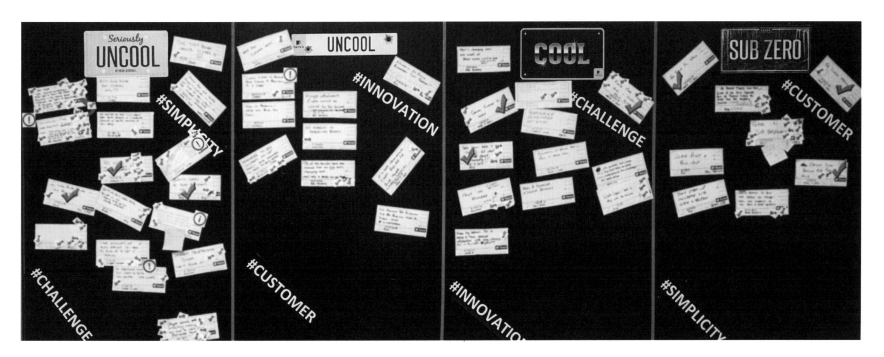

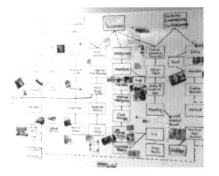

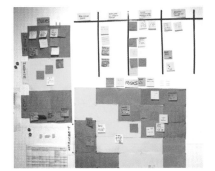

innovation, and interaction with people from all over the business. That would make it a channel for permeation.

I now have this where I currently work and it provides a forum for making key decisions. It is in constant use and spans a number of critical initiatives. Obeya is the forgotten poor cousin of the lean world but one which is vital to overall process. The biggest obstacle in most companies is finding a room!"

Academy Wall

Remember the golden rule of **flow** is that learning often means capturing the way a group shapes information to serve customer needs.

Most organisations treat learning as a dish they serve cold to employees by way of conference attendance, workshops, or webinars. This is so stale it's unpalatable. People assimilate partial information from hundreds of sources (meetups, jams, websites, wikipedia, blogs of every description, authoritative magazines, social media, and so on). The most useful thing you can now do is shape this information through good interaction. And just as you use a pen and paper to sketch out ideas, you can use Walls, especially the Academy Wall, to give shape to the incredible flow of information around you.

An example of what goes onto the Academy Wall comes from what we call Friday Story.

Reflecting publicly on project issues is important but it harbours dangers, especially in Agile. We are opposed to Retrospectives, a technique that Agile adherents use to reflect on what has gone wrong on a project. Retrospectives often exist to blame people.

In place of those, we give people an opportunity to tell stories. One key story technique is Sail Boat (see Chapter 11). Sail Boat is a less threatening way to expose the shortcomings and errors of a project and to identify the key learnings that can go onto the Academy Wall.

Equally, we like to see routine evaluations of cool tools and workarounds. These can be taken off the Cool Wall and their owners asked to tell a story about how they have used them successfully. The team then gets to vote on whether a cool tool should become part of the overall mix of techniques for securing value.

There are other Walls. Companies need a Wall where they expose the stage of cultural transformation. They need a Wall which keeps options in front of them, as not all projects are going to go through the IT shop to delivery. And companies need a Wall where they can see the status of their overall transformation from legacy systems to the right-hand column of our Culture Wall in Chapter 2. But so far, we have just given you a taste and a good starting point.

What does all this add up to?

In many work environments, people assume that a degree of structure, in the traditional sense of the word, will guarantee quality and delivery. But structures as we have known them require a lot of planning, agreement, and sign off.

The fact is that we are are moving at such a fast pace now on many fronts that there isn't the time to create plans and update them in the old way. You need to be in the flow. And, to recap, that means:

- Everyone's eyes are on all tasks, and your team can alert you when the architecture or communications are looking frail.

- You can easily switch out tasks on the Wall when expectations and needs change on a project.

- Your team is made up of people who are comfortable with ambiguity. (We should note, however, that most people won't come to you with this trait fully developed. They'll have to learn as they go, and it's your job to help them by creating a supportive work environment that teaches them to excel at real-time planning in the face of uncertainty.)

- You have your team's attention and engagement. After all, they're the ones who will spot mistakes, see new and different solutions, and suggest improvements.

More than anything else, you need a flexible system that lets you easily integrate what the team learns. This integration should happen not just online but at conferences, in conversation with startups, and while bumping into others at the Wall.

We all have to admit that we are a work in progress and just go with the flow.

Making it work in practice
THE SEARCH FOR PROCESS ON THE PROJECT WALL

Companies are all about processes or "ways to get things done." There is a debate in some areas of IT right now over whether in fact companies do need processes. Leaders at the streaming-video service Netflix argue that smart employees will always find the best way to do things. Companies introduce "process" when they lack real talent.

Netflix believes process is in fact a consequence of growth. As you increase your hiring you need more and more control mechanisms because you take in people who are naturally less autonomous.

This is a fascinating proposition. It acknowledges precisely what we say, that many areas of work are entirely new to everyone. You cannot have a process that lays down the how-to for something nobody has done before. All you can have, or more significantly, the power of what you can do is to unleash people to experiment and find the right way to work, at low cost.

But that in itself is a process. So, the "no-process" argument will always fall down even though process-lite companies can argue that setting guide rails for smart people to work freely within is very powerful.

We argue that the more you can make visible, the more chance you have of capturing the best ideas from the talent you have. For as long as work is hidden in laptops you cannot interact around it. When it is up on the walls, it generates discussion. It becomes a focal point for intelligent social interaction.

For that reason we have emphasised visualisation over and over. Visualisation is a process, of course. More importantly it is also a meeting place. The benefit of visualised processes is that people can talk about them and co-decide what will work and what might not.

In today's firms we see more and more new technologies, techniques or tools being introduced - microapps, microservices, AI, big data and so on. All these require an old process to be replaced by something new. They require process redesign. That becomes an opportunity to loosen the reins as well as give people the power to decide how to work.

By and large we have confined our visualisations to customer segmentation, customer interaction, strategy and portfolio management, project definition and work allocation, and social interactions around jobs, appreciation and learning.

However, the same techniques is useful when it comes to mapping out how new technologies might be introduced. We produced such a visualisation for firms adopting Artificial Intelligence and Machine Learning.

It is relevant to the discussion earlier on Digital Business Walls.

If marketers and developers are to collaborate successfully, as they need to in AI projects, they have to combine their skills in order to redesign processes.

In many companies, over the past decade, new technologies such as social media have failed to bring IT and the business together even though success depends on cooperation.

The newer generation of technologies, such as AI and the Internet of Things, are going to prove very difficult if they do not act as a venue for internal collaboration (and actually for internal-external collaboration).

Visualisations of process can also help shape how internal development projects function (developers know where their work might fit into a new process), or point the way to the right tech partnerships (securing cooperation with strong startups that are more expert), or a combination of these.

Visualisation can help people to design processes for a major innovation like AI.

By laying out the steps visually, we can debate whether the company can add value or not through its internal resources or whether there are shortcuts or whether there are micro-outsourcing options available that can accelerate innovation.

In the visualisation you see here, we have simplified the AI adoption process to give marketers and developers a point of focus. You'll see the four major steps at the top, each with its own subsidiary activities. In fact, any one of these could be broken down again (and will be as the marketers and developers discuss an AI-adoption program).

With a skeleton visualisation like this, the door is open for marketers and developers to get out their Post-it notes and embellish, enlarge, and expand. In the process, they will be reaching agreement on what needs to be done to build a custom process around AI for their company's particular needs.

There are additional elements to puzzles like this. AI has strong ethical implications, such as where one might retain human agency or what are the appropriate uses of customer data. One of the first things good firms do is use those ethical issues to set guide rails for the adoption team.

On the Digital Business Wall, we advocate simple steps to get people going:

- Study new processes at other workplaces. It's rare to be the first to create a new process from scratch. For this one we interviewed 30 executives on their AI-adoption plans and a number of practitioners on how they were going about adoption.

- Create the visualisation as a work in progress. It's never finished but it's a place people can rally around to see and discuss what's emerging.

- Use the major blocks to identify partner opportunities. Will you ever be great at data normalisation? Probably not, but there are people out there who live and breathe it. Can you really devise a watertight AI-adoption business case? Perhaps, but there may be someone who can do it better.

In our world we use visualisations to build the social interactions that surface these options. When you have innovations that have dozens of new steps, as AI does, no leader will be able to produce a foolproof plan for it. By walking hand in hand, however, everyone can lend a hand in making life better.

VISUALISING AN ADOPTION PROCESS FOR AI

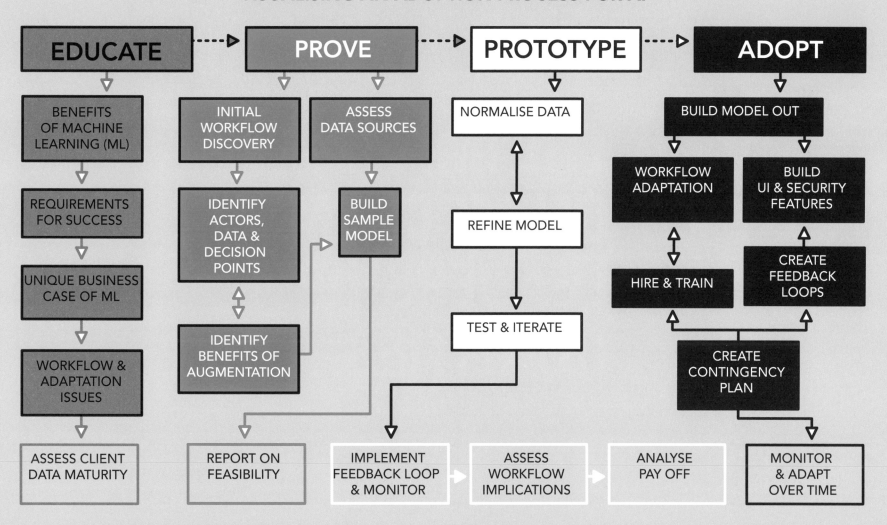

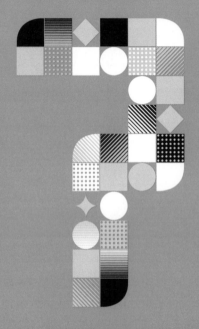

THE IMPACT ON MODERN LEADERSHIP QUALITIES

THERE IS NOW A NEW CADRE OF LEADERS WHO HAVE GONE THROUGH THE TRANSFORMATION PROCESS A FEW TIMES.

They owe nothing to the old school of management or the MBA. They didn't learn any of it at Harvard or INSEAD or the London Business School. They know today's truism from experience: To lead is to inspire trust and belief in a better workplace.

Most important, these people have led an organisation through a specific process of transition where uncertainty rules and a challenge to the status quo is unavoidable. And while there are only a few of these types now, the number is steadily growing into a distinct breed that understands what's needed to fundamentally change organisational processes.

Process change might mean going from waterfall to Agile, in the tech space, or from Agile to DevOps and continuous delivery. In marketing, it could mean shifting from old demographic segmentation to data-driven self-service, pull marketing, or markets of one. In the finance function, it could be new levels of liquidity oversight or even taking on the role of the transaction engine for other businesses (as Apple does for its developers and content providers).

The people who create these transformations have entered the ranks of "experts in management by uncertainty".

A sign of their success is that they will have taken away many of the crutches that allow people to do just enough to get by during the workday. Most of the time that means getting rid of the capacity to stare into a screen without being accountable to one's peers.

They will have successfully raised the demands the organisation makes on people in work by encouraging creativity to be an integral part of how they interact and by building it into process via visualisation.

They will have figured out how to make an enjoyable and rewarding experience out of changing what we do for eight hours by setting the scene for more fun interactions.

Critically, they will have won the level of commitment and belief that makes work more enjoyable; they will have done this by turning over the workspace to employees.

In the process they will have dealt with huge resistance, suspicion from some fellow executives, confrontation with the CEO, and failures that come close to costing the change-makers their jobs.

Leaders who go through this experience a couple of times learn a huge amount about people and even more about their own role.

Like what?

Here are few common traits of leaders for change and transformation.

THE LEADER'S BASELINE PRINCIPLES

Fostering real belief

Most leaders shirk away from the very idea of belief. They duck and dive when it comes to employees building a strong belief in them. They can cope with organisation, planning, and administration but not this intangible, the moment when someone actually looks up to them.

Team members want leadership, not instructions. They want inspiration, not a harassed individual who is projecting their own self-importance back to the team. They want somebody to unlock their career and someone who will listen and guide.

Jeff Immelt, CEO at GE, is a leader who has come in for more than his share of criticism. Yet, he helped promote Beth Comstock to the position of Vice-Chair of the GE Board after appointing her as a young female CMO, breaking the glass ceiling inside the old industrial giant. He began appearing at conferences in jeans and an open-neck shirt alongside developers and startup CEOs. And he has espoused modern platform business strategies that are arguably not exactly on point but are good enough to warrant praise. Here is a leader of a huge company taking time to show he is one of the guys and that he understands how and why change matters.

Being a peer is important. Tim Cook coming out as gay was an incredible move that showed us diversity thrives at the world's most valued company. Not surprising you might argue. Apple is West Coast and hip, of course he would come out. But Cook was in his late 50s before he dared take that step. The point is that, like Immelt, Cook is a late-middle-aged man who realised how incredibly important it is to demonstrate change through personal decision taking.

The day a leader's credibility shines through, she will have people looking up to her. It is scary because at that point, team members have expectations. It's also intimidating because having people believe in you is a burden of responsibility, where R=E, Emotion :-), not a playbook.

Modern leaders don't shirk the responsibility of people's belief. They are comfortable with emotion.

Being the recruiter

"In my last CTO role," says Fin, *"I spent about half my time recruiting for the team. It turned into the most time-consuming job I had, but it was worth every minute, as this is how you create cultural change. I needed to know that these were people who had the talents and temperament to work with minimal supervision yet could also engage in plenty of interaction with their peers. They needed to be people who were comfortable with uncertainty and transparency. And they were really talented people too!*

I wanted them to trust me through what could be difficult times. They had to trust me to make work fun, too. And remember, these were exceptional people, so their trust wasn't easy to win.

Getting it right means these new employees become your recruiters, too. They tell friends and they spread the reputation you want to build. And in some funny sense, being a bit of an emotional person, I do think of them as my team."

Similar sentiments were expressed to us recently by Neal Cross, former head of innovation at Mastercard, who is now at DBS Bank in Singapore.

"We recruit out of places like Google and Amazon," Neal told us. *"We have no problem recruiting. For us, there is no talent shortage. The bank makes a lot of its ambition to be the world's most innovative bank, and people ping me because they want to work with me."*

That's what's now happening around the world. Companies wanting to move fast and having the kind of leadership to make change happen are magnets for talent.

So it is not just about a leader taking on the recruiter role, but also he or she and the organisation earning a reputation for being desirable to work with.

Be the person people crave to work with to advance their careers.

Foster the language of possibility

One of the ways to get leadership right is to foster the language of possibility. There is a tendency, especially in modern startups, to overstate what you are trying to do or what you want to achieve. It's about changing the world, right! Idealism comes easy when you have nothing to lose.

There is a bigger picture, though, in that reacting skeptically to new ideas is somehow built into most of us.

The reaction against an idea emanates from our frameworks and those assumptions we talked about earlier. A good idea challenges the coherence of a belief system. When we react negatively to a new idea, we are usually implying that, against the background of our own assumptions and beliefs, the idea is wacky or plain wrong—by which we mean disturbing and uncomfortable. We judge it as having a low probability of success.

This word probability is so important; it is a mathematical expression. It says something like this: In the majority of cases **x,** the probability that **y** will happen is **z%**. These calculations are always observationally derived. Somebody has looked at the occurrence of **x** and measured the number of **y** instances. Proven, factual, done deal.

We use the term loosely in business, and usually the word we actually mean is not probability but **possibility**. When we hear a new, counter-intuitive idea we are really saying, "I don't like the sound of that possibility." But what we actually say is it's probably not going to work.

Leaders must learn to express themselves positively when they talk about possibilities. They must eschew the very notion of false probabilities. They should accept that many new things are possible and that the enterprise needs to experiment. So the reaction to a new idea, as we said earlier, should be, "Intriguing possibility. How can we test that?"

Dump the false prophets of probability and talk about what is possible.

Resisting the grand scheme of things

A closely related problem is that boards of directors and CEOs want to see the full grand plan written up with a high rate of return attached to it. This is a difficult demand to resist.

People in charge of resources have a right to expect that a major budget request will be accompanied by something that spells out the gains.

On the other hand there is little in the job that is so dispiriting as going home at night to fill in a plan with some hopeful and essentially fake numbers put down only to please the system.

"Fail fast, fail cheap," or Lean innovation, is hopeless as an answer in those situations. You are not going to get the time to build anything small and iterate it upwards.

That's why we have said repeatedly that success comes down to having options in the pipeline. Optionality means building things that might not see the light of day but it also means being prepared. Companies typically resist this notion. In **flow** systems work is broken down into sufficiently small packages that it is possible and indeed imperative to run experiments all the time, building options for what might advance customer satisfaction. A part of many plans is being cooked all the time.

Good leaders create options within their existing budgets and have them ready for prime time when an ROI looks ripe for the taking. Case in point? Apple's iPad was ready before the iPhone. The market just needed to catch up.

Free up resources by Walking the Wall but as well keep building up small plans within the flow.

Being visible about learning

Running into the CIO or CTO at a tech meetup is the kind of thing that shows employees they are in a learning organisation.

"I am always very visible about my learning needs," says Fin. *"I read a lot, I tweet, I attend tech meetups and hackathons, and I give speeches that I need to revise for. There's no point in people looking to me as the guy who knows it all or who knows more than my team members. Both of those are impossible objectives for me to aspire to. I can't know more than most of my teams. I certainly am not the guy who is on top of every topic in tech. I can, however, lead by one very important example: I am always willing to learn."*

Be visibly the best learner in the team.

Being a good or at least willing teacher

In **flow** teams, everyone is a researcher, teacher, and student. As a leader, you have to be those things, too.

Many leaders feel they are too busy to take a moment to teach colleagues. Dismissing the needs of other people when you have a busy schedule is one of the perverse perks of power. But use it at your peril. If you believe taking time to teach is beneath you, if you imagine you have more important things to do and see yourself as too much in a hurry, stop and ask yourself why these people should even bother with you? Yes, you can issue orders, and there will always be sidekicks who can apologise on your behalf when you rush to the next meeting. But you gain that all important belief by what you can mentor in other people.

You have to find time to teach people and to show them you believe that teaching and learning is an important part of your job.

Be a proud teacher.

Outside foot forward, a keystone of what you stand for

In 2016, the English rugby team were transformed by one simple rule: their backline was told to stand with their outside foot forward.

The effect of that was to ready them for the challenge ahead. Leading with the other, inside, foot meant they were always tending to run away from the challenge; you drift, physically and mentally, across the field of play.

Our "outside-foot-forward" mantras are twofold.

The first is the most confrontational.

When in the middle of projects, we always need to ask, "What is the value for the end customer?" We need to ask that with every piece of work, and if we don't know the answer, we're wasting our time. The customer is the value driver.

The second is, "It's not about the person, it's about the profession." In other words, teams need to be critical of each other's professional work without being hurtful to one another.

Develop some simple mantras.

Not shirking the tears

It is difficult to get this balance right. But consider the visual process we discussed in the last chapter. By creating a highly visible work environment, you can help mitigate emotional problems. As well as raising issues, people thank colleagues, offer tips and tricks, and say what's cool and what's not on a wall somewhere in the office.

In our workspaces, there is emotion coursing through the corridors. We can't back away from it so we have to recognise it has many dimensions and give expression to that. We will talk later about giving feedback without causing distress but in simple terms, creating conditions where a variety of emotions can play out, in place of criticism and anxiety, is a tribute to the good, as well as a criticism of the poor, things we do.

Take responsibility for people's emotions.

Visualise small gains

In knowledge work, what we do is often invisible until the day we make mistakes in public. That's why in **flow** we place so much emphasis on visualisation and, in particular, visualising the small gains. These are the wins that keep people coming back and trying harder. Some companies pride themselves on a kind of ruthlessness. Bill Gates was famous for how fiercely he interrogated people to sanity-check their plans. At Google, you are laughed out of the room if you don't have the data to back up your case.

There is another way. In any team or office space, there are small details that someone has given their time and attention to. And the chances are, if they are smart and introspective, their work will not blip on your radar. Visualising work gives us a chance to celebrate these people, too. Use the daily stand-up to communicate wins to everyone on the team as well as bringing risks and issues to the surface so everyone is aware of their responsibilities.

Remember, everything matters to someone.

Putting the goals of the company first

In a workforce now dominated by millennials, it can be tempting to put people first, since, as a culture, we are now obsessed with creating millennial-friendly workplaces. But it is also important to remind people they are there primarily for the collective, which is the company. Encouraging people to embrace the company mission is plain good sense.

Avoid talking about the company as if it is a third party. The company is us.

Taking on the team's fears

Here's Fin on confronting fear:

"In team-building sessions, I always want to talk about the Moose on the table (or Elephant in the room). Is it other people? Sometimes. But often, the Moose is something obvious but unspoken. It is a fear that the organisation will not be supportive of change, even though it is demanding it. Budgets might be inadequate or uncertain, for example, or key innovations might get torched.

As the leader, it is my role to address those concerns, especially when there is this potential for an absurd contradiction: want change, won't pay. Entrepreneurs are effectual leaders, and that means being able to manage all kinds of resources, even when they are in short supply. We have to be that type of entrepreneur internally. If the organisation cannot afford some of the activity we are interested in pursuing, it is up to me to provide alternatives and to be adept at pulling resources from where I can because of my abilities and relationships. As a leader, one has to take that on and not instinctively hide behind adverse decisions about budgets."

Don't hide from the difficult decisions that go against the team either. You are the company.

Setting the guidelines

Most teams can work well within guide rails rather than being forced to follow a playbook. Netflix, for example, has a very delegated form of management. However, they also have very clear guidelines for how projects should run. Managers are encouraged to experiment, test, and run with the evidence, all in the name of better customer experiences.

But not every company is in Netflix's operational mode, growing a global, digital market with a low-price service relative to the competition.

For many of us, the big deal is legacy—changing old systems around, dealing with structures that have been in place for decades or longer, and battling tradition and inertia. That's why we said earlier it is important to bring the customer in to get an idea of how they now behave.

We advocate an experimental environment where testing is critical and data is an excellent basis for some decisions. But what's also important is to get the culture of hypotheses working and play down the current vogue for failure.

Your guide rails should emphasise experimentation, not failure; constantly producing hypotheses to test; and the idea of natural attrition as alternatives to fail fast, fail cheap.

IN SUMMARY
THE LEADERS BASELINE PRINCIPLES

Dump the false prophets of probability and talk about what is possible.

Develop some simple mantras, like: "Avoid getting work done, in favour of getting the *right* work done."

Emphasise experimentation, not failure; constantly produce hypotheses to test; and talk of natural attrition as alternatives to fail fast, fail cheap.

Remember, everything matters to someone.

Don't shirk the responsibility of people's belief. To be successful people need to believe and trust you.

Avoid talking about the company as if it is a third party. The company is us.

Take responsibility for people's emotions.

Don't hide from the difficult decisions that go against the team either. You are the company.

Be a proud teacher.

Be visibly the best learner in the team.

Be the person people crave to work with to advance their careers.

Free up resources by Walking the Wall but as well keep building up small plans within the flow.

ORGANISING THE FIRST *FLOW* TEAM

IT'S NOW TIME TO FORGE THE TEAMS THAT ARE GOING TO DELIVER A BETTER PLACE TO WORK, AND WE MEAN BETTER IN EVERY SENSE: MORE FUN, MORE PRODUCTIVE, AND CREATING MORE VALUE FOR CUSTOMERS.

What you need for your first **flow** team is a group of leaders who can pass on the spirit of **flow** to the teams around them. More than just being evangelists for the company, they should be able to take on the task of figuring out with colleagues how work must change now that economies are being constantly disrupted, not least by the pace of process innovation. Walls can help. This newbie team, if they are worth their salt, will quickly pick up on the reasons that visual work is so effective.

SCALE, SCOPE, SPEED

One of the elephants in the room in large organisations, or the moose that sits on the table, is fragmentation. That's the blast of icy air we talked about in Chapter One that begins by shattering the old massively dysfunctional world of large IT systems (RIP).

Fragmentation has many worthwhile aspects in the workplace, not least that it reflects the new, wider scope of value you can deliver to customers by being faster and more entrepreneurial. The wider the scope you have in offering products, services and features, the closer you get to providing what people really want. But it means more work.

There are three aspects to fragmentation:

- Modern infrastructure allows us to manage a practically limitless number of endpoints, which tends to drive change towards more highly scaled markets.

- Modern consumers want experiences and services that suit their individual needs. Change is therefore invariably about scope and choice for the end consumer.

- Consumers want improvement at speed.

Every company needs to set their objectives against the backdrop of these three elements: **scale**, **scope**, and **speed**.

How does this play out in practice? Let's take the insurance industry as an example.

In the insurance industry, scale, scope, speed might mean redesigning systems so that the company can offer a more fragmented—that is, a more diverse and personalised— product suite. So, instead of one undifferentiated car policy for everyone between 25 and 60, the company takes advantage of digitally delivered data to offer products for people with a particular driving style. Imagine, for example, having data on driving speeds and braking habits. The insurance company might then reduce coverage for people driving between midnight and 4.00 am, to discourage exposure to the danger of drunk drivers, or charge a premium when the car is driven at those times by people with a pattern of aggressive driving.

Those types of considerations are very much about the Amazon effect—giving new choices and correlating that with more creative pricing. It is doable today because computing systems can manage billions of endpoints in the form of data, customers, transactions, etc.

The origins of fragmentation lie in our new ability to manage these infinite endpoints. Systems are now designed with limitless management capability in mind. Managing 1,000 different products, services, and customer categories is not exponentially more complex than managing 10. Supporting a customer base of 2 billion is now as possible as managing 100,000 users used to be.

The other factor at work, of course, is the empowered consumer. People are less and less likely to want to pay for all the elements of a generic service because they have stronger ideas about what they want. Spread across modern lifestyles, there are many instances where we subsidise others or overpay for functionality we don't use. People are fed up with this.

In auto-insurance, I might resent paying policy premiums that really support poor, sometimes mindless driving by other road users. I think I deserve some reward for avoiding the commuter jam. I would be happy for telematic data from my car to go to an insurer because it would show how carefully I brake.

Finally, the trend towards more variegated services takes place at a faster pace. We already pointed out the incredible innovation rate at Skyscanner. Corporations are now beginning to resemble craft mechanics, fine-tuning the delivery of services in real-time. This is going to become more pronounced as AI and machine learning automate more innovation. In sum, after forty years of computing, we now really know how to do it well!

So part of change means embracing scale, scope, and speed.

In the context of this fragmentation, innovation assumes a very different hue. Those mandates—creativity, product innovation, and system change—spell out only part of what is needed.

In the past, we have thought of product innovation as a series of one-off events. Google Glass, mentioned earlier, is a good example. After all was said and done, the product was just a heads-up display made to look geeky. The same goes for inventing an air bubble for a new training shoe or creating a new suitcase wheel. This is trivial in a technology sense.

Old business processes assume the ability to gather market data, change the raw material of a product, and add something new.

The great companies like Procter and Gamble did this continuously with innovations. Take, for example, the improvement of coldwater enzymes that allowed for cooler temperatures in the washing machine and a value proposition around energy saving. This is standard innovation fare.

Today, the innovation process is a based on a continuous, highly adaptive, **internal workflow**. Your advantage comes less from product innovation (though, yes, new products are great) and more from **process-model innovation**.

In the mind of traditional innovators, process-model innovation takes a backseat but here's a way to look at things in a different light:

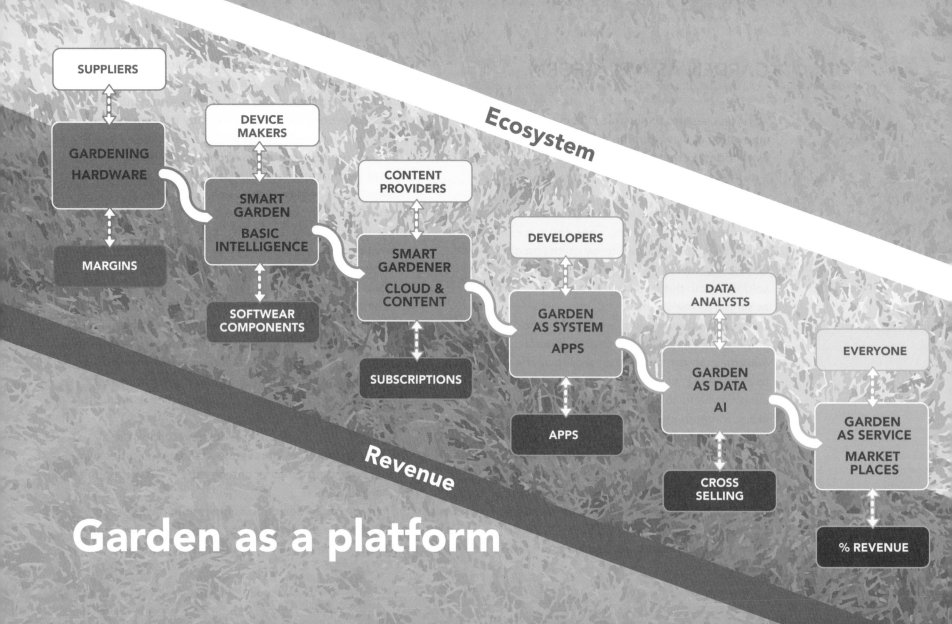

GARDEN AS A PLATFORM

Haydn uses this to illustrate the current range of innovation activity and the range of process models at work today. Let's look at your garden as if it were part of a business platform.

Think of the supply chain that provides the local garden centre with spades, hoes, forks, sprinklers, and seeds. Much of that used to be quite straight forward. Garden centres imported products from China and sold them on. But let's look at changes to something as simple as the sprinkler.

Recent innovations in this space have added some intelligence to this simple device—beginning with an automatic on-off switch and ranging all the way up to automating water dosing, dependent on ambient conditions and soil type. These have given us something like automated irrigation and in the process expanded the supplier ecosystem to include device makers and software writers as well as introducing more revenue possibilities.

Now imagine that you, the gardener, are unwittingly cultivating the wrong type of plant for your soil type and humidity levels. You need a smart-garden system to go along with the connected sprinkler. And it would be very much based around content about flowers, vegetables, seeds and maintenance. The system may come in the form of a cloud-based application that would guide you through the content stack intelligently by learning your tastes, location, and interpreting the need for water from sensors in your garden. It could then help you choose better plants for your soil type and climate.

Behind changes like these lies a significant shift in supply from dumb tools to connected devices and to content and data for both the sprinkler system and the gardener.

If your old sprinkler supplier provides the smart system, she will inevitably have gravitated work processes away from importing watering roses and rubber tubing from China. She will have hired a bunch of software developers and content creators, and will be contracting for cloud storage and processing power. She will also be looking closely at data and will have hired a few specialists to program a personalisation aspect into the application.

Now the sprinkler supplier is starting to look like a platform and sources of revenue are expanding because she charges for premium content and carries ads on the portal and app.

Then she might decide to augment her own dosing app with some third-party apps that connect the various elements of the garden (e.g., the lighting system to your energy control and security systems) with data collection, image recognition software, and possibly some AI. This is sophisticated stuff. She charges developers for access to the customer data she has accumulated and now your sprinkler supplier is a transaction engine distributing app purchase fees to the developers. Most likely she will be charging a small fee for the software development kit that app developers use.

Now, what if part of your problem with this garden is a lack of time on your part? Your sprinkler supplier might see that as an opportunity for a marketplace. There are plenty of senior citizens nearby who would love to pass a couple of hours a day tending to your garden.

To get to this point, your sprinkler supplier will have invited a wide cross section of people and skills into the process of watering your garden and giving you better plants. To do this at speed, she will undoubtedly have followed the processes we are talking about in this book. Everybody involved, once you get past the rubber and metal, is creating something new, relying on social interaction to hypothesise and then judge what the market for smart gardeners will bear.

In the same way, modern business critically hangs on the process transitions that take us from product to app to data, platform, ecosystem, intelligence, and marketplaces at pace.

Many of the gains from **process-model innovation** come from how teams interact and the context you set. High-performance capability, with this wide range of revenue sources, and complex ecosystems, requires thinking differently. Against the backdrop of DevOps and microservices, it means securing support for quite profound process innovation in the context of speed in delivery.

This is what you want to excite your teams about. You need people who can take a big bite of this loaf of change and love the taste.

THE TWO EDGES OF INNOVATION

Innovation today is rooted in intangibles like attitude, co-creation, data, learning, and feedback. All this adds up to the capacity to deliver a more and more fine-tuned level of service appropriate to each user's needs and wallets.

People whose primary orientation is the outward-facing business need—strategy, sales, and marketing—still tend to believe a new product will give them the edge in every market they touch.

In reality, they are often not comfortable with new products. Give them something they've never seen before and they are likely to say, "But we already know what sells!" Rarely integrated into innovation processes, they are typically incentivised to sell yesterday's products. And often, they do it well.

The first principle of a **flow** team is that sales and marketing must be a part of it, along with business analysts, developers and anyone else involved with the project. All areas of business need to gravitate towards software. The old idea that the requirements for this could be handed over to developers needs to be put in a coffin and buried.

The other side of innovation is the new process models. Note Murphy's new law. Before worrying about screwing up, remember there are few processes that can remain fixed for very long.

In the past, processes stayed in place for decades or even centuries. For example, the way fleet managers service cars didn't change for fifty years until telematics and AI allowed for preemptive servicing. The way banks offer mortgages has more or less involved the same processes since the 1980s.

But it is impossible today to meet customer needs in this way. Instead:

- You need processes that emphasise scale, scope, speed.

- You cannot let up on process-model innovation. How you deliver will be as open to change as what you deliver.

Take, for instance, companies like Uber and Airbnb. Their basic product or service is an app and a transaction engine to manage money flows.

Apart from the convenience of the app, and maybe a transient price advantage, these companies offer the market little more than what is already there. The key to their success is that they do it at scale, with scope, and at speed.

Everything that they do is built on this foundation, right? Well, sort of. But "foundation" is the wrong metaphor when we're talking about **flow** and modern work. We think of foundations as solid, stationary starting points that aren't supposed to evolve.

By contrast, today's "foundation" for most companies must be a constantly changing flow of software, hardware, data, and communications.

For some, physical products are still essential. Rolls Royce Aerospace, for example, still has to make engines. It needs engineers who know how to calibrate the alloys and engine size to get better performance.

However, even they now sell "Miles in the Sky", or how long an engine will keep flying before it needs to be grounded for maintenance. They sell a concept that requires constant adaptation in order to improve.

In other words, the long-awaited service economy is arriving at warp speed. And it is defined by the characteristics we have just outlined.

SETTING UP THE FIRST FLOW TEAM

Our definition of innovation tells you why **flow** teams are so important. They have to deal with all the transitions and novelty described above. Here are the steps towards forming that team.

Convey a vision of disruption

You have to convey some of the turbulence that's taking place in your market. At the very least, you need to convey how you see the external environment changing. Your real focus is on what to change internally but the reason for that is out there. If you don't have a view of what's changing in the economy externally, and why the new ways of work you want to discuss are the right response, what else will you begin with?

Create the skills' profiles

A lot of people approach skills' needs with platitudes like, "I need team players". As we saw earlier, teams need people who can quickly learn how to be be open, respectful, and capable of listening. But they also need the kind of expertise that goes with being hard-working and more than moderately gifted in a particular area (such as business analysis and work breakdown).

The people you need will take a limited set of tasks and redesign them **into the flow.** The team needs to be inclusive but should have one over-riding competency:

Members can accept that the plan will emerge through their interaction, creating a degree of uncertainty that might be new to them.

Key personal characteristics

People who thrive within **flow** teams are typically believers in the new stystem. But unbelievers are vital, too, to ensure that course correction is swift when things start to go wrong. (Ironically, they quickly become believers themselves when the team gets some real tangible runs on the board.)

The initial ambiguity of starting up the **flow** will soon be forgotten when the team reaches the right cadence

KEY MEMBER TYPES

Executive

Strategist who will keep the project on the Executive Wall.

An executive who will interact with the team as a peer rather than a boss.

Prepared to ensure the team and project can resist isolation.

Voice of the customer

Someone who lives and breathes the idea of value for the customer - it could even be a customer.

People who will interact with the data with an open mind; seek new relevant data but be subtle about introducing the idea of errors being made.

Market segmentation skills.

Empiricist

Someone who loves the detail and seeks the proof points; skilled at problem disaggregation.

First in line to organise testing and evaluation of any idea.

The work breakdown specialist.

Enabler

A person who knows how to keep conversations going rather than close them down.

The one who is keen to make the new work process fun.

People who are capable of adapting the go-live process, imagineering how the newer system parts are going to supercede what is already in place.

Creative

Sees the big picture 3 - 5 years out; skilled in system adaptation at a high level, constantly learns about the main trends.

People who can see how the **flow** will reform into something different without being 100% sure.

People who are happy to noodle out the connections between dozens of different options and developments.

or predictable pace. **Flow** facilitates quick delivery and hence stops negativity from seeping in.

However, from time to time, a toxic team member emerges and a true leader has to ensure that the person does the best work of their career—somewhere else.

But toxicity is rare and is usually driven by people who believe the world is flat or that Waterfall is Agile.

Apart from that, a true **flow** team must always be inclusive. No one characteristic or skill is better than another, because everyone is different and diversity is richer than having a team of replicants. The extroverts will drive the process and the introverts will help ensure the proper guide rails are in place and respected. The happy people will celebrate success and the angry people will have nothing to complain about!

Communicating vision

The message to the first flow team is:

"We have a new vision in this company. We know that all customer requirements ultimately boil down to granularity and value. We want to respect the changing needs of existing customers and provide services in a way that will attract new ones."

"We require a new kind of flexibility. We are going to work differently but won't always know what that means. We are entitled to invent process and workflow."

Creating purpose with a single sentence

The team needs to co-create a one-sentence summary of the purpose of this team of new leaders. The purpose statement should also be capable of imparting a sense of adventure. It's only possible to finalise the statement once you go through the rest of the steps. In later **flow** teams, this statement will be attached to specific objectives but for now it can be something simple like, "Let's collaborate on discovering a new way to create value" or "Our goal is to eliminate friction by minimising handovers in the organisation." In IT specifically, it could be "Our goal is to redesign the architecture so that we can do microservices". For marketing, it's "Our goal is to build the best Go To Market model imaginable so we can enhance our product innovation outputs".

Being open about who is on the team and why

One of the first discussions should be about who is

on the team and why they are there. What attributes do they have that matter? As the **flow** principles permeate the team, it becomes a critical insight for people to know why they are there and to build belief and a sense of responsibility around the adventure. "We have chosen you because you have shown yourself to be very open or adaptable" is a great thing for an employee to hear.

Putting boundaries on the team's scope of work

Teams that have been selected because they are comfortable with uncertainty still actually need boundaries. It's important they realise they won't change the world, or even the company, with a single project. Without boundaries, the team will overreach, tread on other people's toes, and maybe become arrogant. Productivity may decrease because people bite off more than they can chew. You are creating a team that wants to achieve great things. Placing boundaries guides and directs them. Nonetheless, the first **flow** team is there to help develop new processes, spread the word, and ultimately guide or be a model for others. These tasks have to be built into the remit of any actual project they engage in.

Making clear how the first flow project relates to company goals

We often use the term "a cog in the wheel" to describe our place in the sytem. Instead, team members today can be part of a beautiful picture like a mosaic or some other analogy that suits your culture. They need to know the role that their piece in the mosaic plays. Take, for example, the initial work breakdown of a new executive priority. As this image of a new priority starts to take form, each person on the team will have a role in defining a step along the way to delivery. They also need an insight into the opportunities that high performance will open up for them during this journey. That's all part of the mosaic.

Identifying the blockers

Every team faces blockers, like routine process issues and poor work methods. Leaders need to get these out in the open. The question you need to address here is "What gets in the way of efficiency, automation and value?"

You are not looking for big picture items like political struggles or elephants in the room. Instead, ask questions like:

- Where are the blockers?

- What do we typically do wrong in our organisation?

- What stops good value creation?

- Are there other executives who distract us with spontaneous demands?

- Is the backlog itself creating a problem of prioritisation?

- Are we worried about resources?

This process allows you to lay out some potential solutions, number one being that from now on we spot blockers early and deal with them quickly.

The moose on the table

Some of the difficult subjects that need addressing are obvious. They are not in the corner of the room hiding. They are there in between everyone. You need to talk about them and, as a leader, take responsibility for addressing them. These are the organisational issues that can derail momentum and motivation. They might be issues like the persistent casual demands of the organisation or the low level of trust in management's commitment to change. Talk about them and agree the right pathway to resolution. Don't promise a miracle but be believable when you say I can solve it **this way...**

Psychological profiling

Always work with a psychologist on this. Good profiling of people's skills and attributes helps a leader to feel more secure in the decisions she is making about who should be onboard and, as important, help anticipate problems down the road. In almost all teams, individuals will have problems that keep them out of work at critical times. It pays to have some upfront awareness so that the potential for emotional or family problems is already factored into your approach to team management. Quite apart from that, it is so important to know what motivates each team member and how best to blend their different working styles. As leaders, few of us have these insights without help from psychologists (though we might believe we are natural-born leaders who are intuitive and ultra smart).

Encourage people to challenge

People have to be willing to challenge each other on efficiency, automation, and value. But they also need to challenge leaders and ignore hierarchy in order to stop us doing something stupid.

But it is never personal. It is professional.

Going through these points in the early formation of a new team helps establish a basis for the personal relationships that are so vital to success. At this stage, it means being able to make exponentially more adaptations to the services your customers receive.

The group in the room with you will be the arrow tip for the early stages of the journey. As time goes on other people in the organisation will learn from how this group has formed and performed.

At the same time you, the leader, are delivering on a promise. That is, you are asking, implicitly, for their belief; in return, you are giving them a high degree of autonomy. You are asking them to be creative and you have offered them a chance to take control of their work.

Remember, too, that sometimes the leader, as the driver of change, is often seen as the moose by the team.

Your **flow** teams are going to create a blueprint for working with uncertainty, fragmentation and constant change.

You are looking for members of these teams to be:

■ Skilled enough to break down processes and workflows, and then reform them in a loosely structured way (using visualisation, which we will talk about next).

■ Confident about communicating errors to each other.

■ Capable of evolving the overall plan for the project.

■ Able to celebrate success.

Here's a comparison that will help with orienting the team and finding the right people for **flow**. Very often, the characteristics on the left are the ones sought after for high-performance teams, sometimes called Tiger Teams. Look at the comparison.

ARE YOU MORE
TIGER OR FLOW?

TIGER TEAM

- MISSION AND GOAL ORIENTED
- SOLVES DISCRETE PROBLEMS
- HIGHLY STRUCTURED RESPONSIBILITIES
- STRONG CONFLICT-MANAGEMENT SKILLS
- FINITE
- COMBATIVE
- STRONG ON TEAM ALIGNMENT

FLOW TEAM

- UNCERTAINTY ORIENTED
- DESIGNING NEW WAYS TO SOLVE PROBLEMS AND DELIVER SOLUTIONS
- CO-CREATES PROCESSES
- INHERENTLY SELF CRITICAL
- PARTICIPATIVE AND EVOLVING
- COMFORTABLE WITH EQUAL SHARE OF VOICE
- SEEKS NOVELTY

CREATING COLLABORATIVE WORK PROCESSES

MOST ORGANISATIONS STRUGGLE WITH WORKFLOW THAT INHIBITS INNOVATION ACTIVITY.

Workflow is control, and control, almost by definition, means having to do things a certain way and by a certain standard. Control is conformity.

Controlled systems cannot, by nature, innovate. That puts them in direct conflict with today's demand for real-time business and creating a culture of innovation. People need permission (or at least need to feel free) to keep changing the system in order to innovate. They need to engage with process-model innovation.

This chapter will examine how **flow** naturally creates a process-design community that supports rapid innovation.

The definition of process is the order in which things get done. Work is usually divided into small chunks. As we said earlier, this chunking has historically been done on Adam Smith's principles: create specialisation and you get efficiency. But in the modern organisation, it's crucial that we stop the drive towards this kind of specialisation and reintroduce the scope for diverse skills, interdisciplinary work, and chopping and changing. That will go hand in hand with teams that form and reform.

Here's an illustration of a trend towards smaller interdisciplinary teams.

AN EXAMPLE FROM TV

In the old days, in Britain, all TV programmes were made either by the BBC or the independent network ITV. Two organisations, lots of rules about how to secure budgets and how to work. For example, you needed a seven-person crew to go out and film something. It was a similar situation in the U.S., where the networks made the programmes and broadcast them to the world (or at least their part of the world).

Within this control system, people were generally quite creative. However, they were bound by a huge amount of rules around who could do what and how many people should be involved.

Then, from the early 1980s onward, the industry moved to a new "publishing" model. New legislation put the networks in the position of publishing houses that commissioned programs from small, independent production companies (some of which eventually became quite large). However, most of those small companies did not even exist at the time of the legislation. It took an entrepreneurial revolution in TV to bring them into being. As a result, the whole system of TV production changed: the managerial hierarchy, comissioning, production systems, team composition, and so on.

We have seen that drift, from oligopoly to diversity, elsewhere, too. Think of the thousands of companies in the app space in mobile or the innovations in photography, which now come from small companies with new AR filters or social features for images, in place of one giant such as Kodak.

In many areas of business, we are moving away from vertically integrated industries to something more like a publishing model, one where larger organisations commission work from smaller ones (or, more pertinently, where smaller ones force themselves onto the larger business agenda).

This means the business agenda—what gets done, when and how fast it happens—is set by nimbler small companies.

In the TV industry, when those small companies began to emerge they had to learn a number of new tricks:

1 **The ideas' factory.** They had to propose many more projects than the old large ones had to, just to see what would stick. Survival depended on becoming ideas' factories. (recognise that?)

2 **Hypotheses as work.** Instead of putting resources towards areas like administration and marketing, work became a process of generating hypotheses about what publishers might buy and how consumers would react.

3 **Fungible roles.** These smaller companies had to accept certain economies in their operations. Film crews, for example, declined in number from around six or seven (cameraman, assistant cameraman, sound engineer, assistant sound engineer, PA, reporter) to, in some cases, a reporter who did her own sound and camera. In other words, roles became more fungible.

4 **More experimental.** Each day became a return to basic process redesign as resources became more dispersed and had to be gathered together anew for each project. That meant asking questions like; "How can we execute on Project X given this level of budget? How do we ensure high-quality and varied locations and the right talent to help us? How do we acquire the resources we need if a broadcaster will not pay all the budget? Who can we call on to do "mates' rates" for a vital part of the shoot?"

A project breakdown would include guesswork about the people who might be involved in the project, the extent of travel and accommodation, interviewees, locations, logistics, and so on.

Each of the following could be a variable:

■ Which director? At what cost? With what availability?

■ The same for other major roles: Which on screen talent? Who to interview?

- How do locations x, y, and z influence travel budgets and logistics?
- How do interviewees a, b, and c affect locations and travel?

The whole operation would be a movable feast. And the entire time that the feast is being cooked, the executive producer will still be securing a production budget, planning distribution channels and partnerships, thinking about marketing, and so on.

Something of this uncertainty has now entered mainstream business. Senior management has become akin to commissioning editors who order up projects for publication.

The big problem that still exists in work, even in Agile, is that we plan for certainty rather than create processes that can manage the uncertainty that we all feel.

The expectation of a solid plan that can be well executed lies at the heart of the business-commissioning process and is reflected in the Agile approach.

Businesses aspire to eliminate uncertainty by putting rigid specifications and roles in place. But in reality, work is returning to its craft roots, where people possess a broader set of skills.

The right analogy for this, if you want to capture **flow** in one static image, is a mosaic: many, many parts that make up the overall picture. We mistakenly try to build the Mosaic on paper before we've any sense of the colour scheme or the narrative, or before a single individual piece has actually been made. The return to craft means letting the team develop those parts of the Mosaic they do really well. Or they can piece together work as and when the needs of the day become discernible.

What we propose in flow is a future state where functions, features, and workflow change in the name of creating better value.

That's also akin to what documentarists do.

They imagine a story arc, then hypothesise which interviewees they can access and what they will say. They storyboard how those interviews might be visualised based on likely responses. Then they try to figure out, in advance, how to move from one segment to another, which also involves predicting the filming locations. All of this is open to variation and redesign.

There is always some tension in an environment built on hypotheses. The commissioning editor wants to be sure she is buying something compelling; the filmmaker is only hypothesising that something compelling lies inside the story they want to tell.

For that reason, a commissioning editor will often provide a development budget, which is a way of saying,

"Go away and get me some proof, then we'll talk."

That's exactly the position we should encourage in all areas of business. We must accept tension as a normal reaction to innovation; give managers power to fund a "prove it" period and then work to an adaptive plan just like a film's shooting script (many of which are re-written dozens of times before they gain credibility).

THE BREAKDOWN

In this section, we will talk about how to break work down similar to the way it is broken down in film, or at least following those principles. In business, we need to break work down to the point where the problems of uncertainty can be better managed while acknowledging we will all live with doubt.

Often, if not always, market and technological uncertainty is exacerbated by the vagaries of project work. We set out on a project and screw it up. Or, as one CIO told us, we tend to start projects happy and end them sad. That sadness is usually a consequence of bloated expectations as the 'sell' is made to the C-Suite, interpersonal rivalries as reality sinks in, and poor management.

We should start projects with a degree of healthy skepticism if we want to end them happy. To put it another way, we should follow the example of some of the great creatives out there and break work down to the point where we have a new degree of control.

On that point, would you have imagined creative people being great planners? Well, Woody Allen storyboards every scene he intends to film and illustrates with detailed sketches every camera angle he is going to use. Very little is left to chance, everything is at a reasonable cost, and everybody knows what is expected of them.

The point is though that it may take a year or more to get to this point. In business we don't have a year. We have to adopt the creative's practice of imagineering at the same time as inventing the methods that will help us to drive value or alternatively leave us in a position to pivot.

We also have other creative constraints:

1 To understand work in enough detail that we can assign novel tasks to one individual that can be completed in a day or two.

2 Through that breakdown to give ourselves access to precise costs and scheduling information (simply a sum of tasks, people, and days).

3 To do that while being guided by what produces customer value fastest and most effectively, with the reverse also being true, that we can cancel or pivot when we sense that value is not being created.

Those needs are best met with an eye on the Pareto Principle that 80 percent of the value can be created by 20 percent of the resources. If we don't embrace these concepts, then work runs away from us and we waste time in painful retrospectives, looking for scapegoats.

In business, we have not traditionally talked about planning as a creative task. Our job has been to follow processes that guarantee a profit. More and more, though, we hypothesise about what will create value—some additional feature or the use of a new technology or a design innovation. And just like the filmmaker, if we are to advance the cause, we need to figure out who can deliver that value, using which tools, surrounded by which people, over what timeframe. And much of this has to be done ahead of the proof. It also has to be done with a sense that we are in control of events. The best way to do that is to get to that magic point we discussed above, sketching out the camera angles (or getting to the smallest piece of work that makes creative sense).

BEYOND EPICS AND STORIES

Agile development in IT uses the language of Epics and Stories to convey the work breakdown process. Epics, as the word suggests, are big. Stories are small.

There are problems, though, with this concept and the language used. Stories are parts of an Epic but stories are still too large to be part of a truly adaptive workflow. They take time to produce and they have to fit precisely with all the other Stories in an Epic. Also, when you look at Epics and Stories, they seem contrived. The desire to tell a User Story is good but it leads to us second-guessing users. Bring users in and let them have access to a version of the Customer Wall.

Instead of this reality check, by and large, User Stories are based on personas, which are fictional composites of people who don't really exist. These composites will be representative of some customer category, hopefully, but in today's world of big data, we can actually understand customer segmentation a whole lot better. And thanks to social media, we can talk to customers all day long if we wish.

In Agile, stories also become essential pillars in an overall plan, which is fine in principle but often problematic in practice. Because stories are generally too large this leads to a variety of issues when a workflow has multiple teams delivering their parts of a project after three weeks of sprints. Yes, they will be on time, they will be fast but will each team's work be relevant to everyone else's?

Scrum/Agile is often equivalent to a second-unit director (the ones who do the action sequences) coming back to the editing site with a totally different tone from the one the main director is creating.

A key to creating good flow is getting the work breakdown right and our understanding of what is right, or more useful, is still evolving. Creatives break work down to the point where their peers can execute their craft. We in business have much to learn from this. We should also bear in mind though that we are asking people to do something entirely new, a demand that only the minority of creative people are faced with.

EATING THE ELEPHANT

Now, back to the issue of creating flow. Most people would baulk at eating an elephant. Elephants are big and tough and hard to fit on a plate. But many organisations still run projects as if they had folks willing to eat the elephant, or, less figuratively, attack a big project and expect to finish it, whenever.

Big-project syndrome automatically creates hierarchy in teams, even in Agile. It hands over responsibility to those with the patience to plan and second guess the future months down the line. That leads to a lot of people being left out of the loop, becoming involved only when they are assigned to a task. The level of social interaction is low and input is constrained to the leader group. This tends to be a folly of Scrum and Agile.

It can be done differently!

THE NITTY GRITTY OF FLOW

You'll remember from earlier that projects pass from the Executive Portfolio Wall down to the Team Kanban Wall but this is done out in the open where everyone can express a view about the work breakdown.

There are good reasons for becoming extremely skilled at this breakdown:

- It resolves conflict often before it begins. Everybody knows what a feature, product, or service will cost. Doubt over resource allocation is a major issue in Agile.

- It is transparent, so internal costings cannot be used as a form of blackmail (as often happens with Agile Sprints, when business managers are told, well, that sprint is really going to cost you).

- It provides an opportunity to get a good sense of timescales because work is designed in two-day blocks.

- It is a great way to get to work allocations that match skills, passions, and tasks.

The skills needed on any given project breakdown will incorporate the ability to identify dependencies (traditionally a project management skill) and the ability to break a project down by its actual value. (Value must be reflected in work that adds value for customers rather by what a manager favours in some way.) The aim is to create a project definition that allows teams to start work quickly, on the most high-value parts of the project.

From this breakdown, the work packages become tasks that can be allocated to the right individuals. But the work tasks have to be under scrutiny too. We need task definition that can be completed in a couple of days max and that won't pose a problem at the point of integration.

The work breakdown also involves the traditional process of looking at work from the perspective of those who will use the product's functions and features.

Flow is not a prescriptive methodology for how work will pass through the system. A key learning about **flow** is to not to take it on as a complete methodology. If you try, you risk cultural rejection, just as you would if you impose a new social business platform or force-feed your developers Agile.

Each organisation will use **flow** differently and even contribute new ideas into it. We find staff very quickly decide to build out visualisations we have never thought about.

It's best for many organisations to start with just one or two of the Walls we discussed earlier. This gets people used to stand-ups. It also introduces transparency, open debate, pivoting in public in ways that are clearly, visibly, not going away. **Flow** is not a vendor product that needs implementing. Rather it becomes an end-to-end system when people embrace it and build it out for themselves.

As we've seen, the Executive Portfolio Wall (which some observers are now calling the key ingredient of a Transformation Program Office) is a great way to engage the C-Suite in the end-to-end process of continuously converting ideas into value. Ideas are laid out for all to see as they traverse the Walls, from inception before becoming "in-play" on a Project Wall.

This is where the heavy lifting begins, and where you need great product owners and superlative business analysts. They will bear the brunt of work breakdown, starting with the Goal.

A single card from the Executive Portfolio Wall is, to all intents and purposes, a "Goal". That Goal needs to be broken into smaller sub-goals (the Epics in Agile) and finally into even smaller tasks, those Stories we talked about earlier but going beyond that to sketch out the camera angles.

Stories should use common English, rather than developer or marketing jargon, to describe what a customer wants. They should also start the process of breaking those wants into the Mosaic pieces that will become features in a product or service.

We begin this on the "Project Wall". This is a great place to see the informality of **flow** because the input is usually something as succinct as a customer tweet or a short message from a team member. The Wall itself can end up being big, depending on the size of the project but its genesis is just one card from the Executive Wall.

Generally, we start with this one Goal.

For instance, we are going to build a new product, as requested by the CMO (or CEO or Board).

The Goal will be split into Epics that can stand on their own but are also closely aligned with one another. Using the movie analogy, the Goal is a pitch, the Epics are the Acts, and the Stories are the scenes. We have to go further though. The new workflow goes as deep as distinct camera Angles as we break stories down.

Each Angle needs to be very independent, succinct, and small, able to be built in less than five days, but preferably in two and, most importantly, easy to test.

Many organisations fail with Agile because they go straight from a Goal to trying to build the Epics, which are often too big. This can lead to a team losing the plot for reasons often unrelated to the developers' skills. For example, when teams deliver, there will be a huge amount of integration needed, which is fine only if everybody is sticking to the Script.

The same goes for Story Angles—they need to be really small. In fact, they need to be uniform in size, because this is the Holy Grail of **flow**: you can estimate cost and timescales with great accuracy from the right breakdown.

For example, 100 Story Angles on the Wall, each taking four days to build, is a 400-day Epic. Multiply that by the number of Epics and then divide by the number of your developers, and you have a launch date for a project.

Epics, Stories, and Story Angles, seem sterile without an essential ingredient: Value. What value does each Story or Story Angle have for the customer?

We have written about value, the practice of always seeking to relate work to a distinct customer outcome, on numerous occasions already. Whilst it's a great skill to write small Story Angles (the pieces in the mosaic) it's an even greater skill to assemble or prioritise them by value. Having analysts that can do this means a project is on its way to success very quickly.

Why? Because to know or identify which stories to build first is a considerable competitive advantage. It leads to outputs being delivered to the end customer quickly, and that means you can immediately start returning revenue or gaining other benefits very early on.

But here's the twist. You don't have to deliver all the Stories and Angles. As little as 20 percent of the stories can drive 80 percent of the value. The best product managers know when they have maximised this so-called Pareto Principle and can move confidently onto the next project from the Executive Wall.

If, on the other hand, managers insist on building every story to completion before the project moves on, they will hog resources and hurt the company in the same way that old, large projects did.

TEAM KANBAN WALLS

So what about Scrum, the jewel in Agile methodology, and the Team Kanban wall?

Well, if you imagine the Executive Portfolio Wall is primarily for execs and the Project Wall is primarily for business users (product managers, analysts etc.), the team Kanban Wall is for work allocation. We should point out that we say "primarily" but of course anyone has access to the Project Wall.

As work is being broken down, the stories are passed on to the software engineers whose work is organised on the Team Kanban Wall.

In Agile, we would now be talking about a Scrum framework where the product owner creates and prioritises a wishlist or backlog that engineering teams then take away to work on. The engineers are usually allocated two to three weeks for completion and meet in regular sprint sessions to assess progress. The project will finish with a retrospective in order to learn lessons and process.

Flow prefers a Team Kanban Wall because it's another step in creating transparency. It allows us to modulate tasks that the team is working on. It's one card per person on this Wall. You can segment a technical wall to have some people assigned to new features and

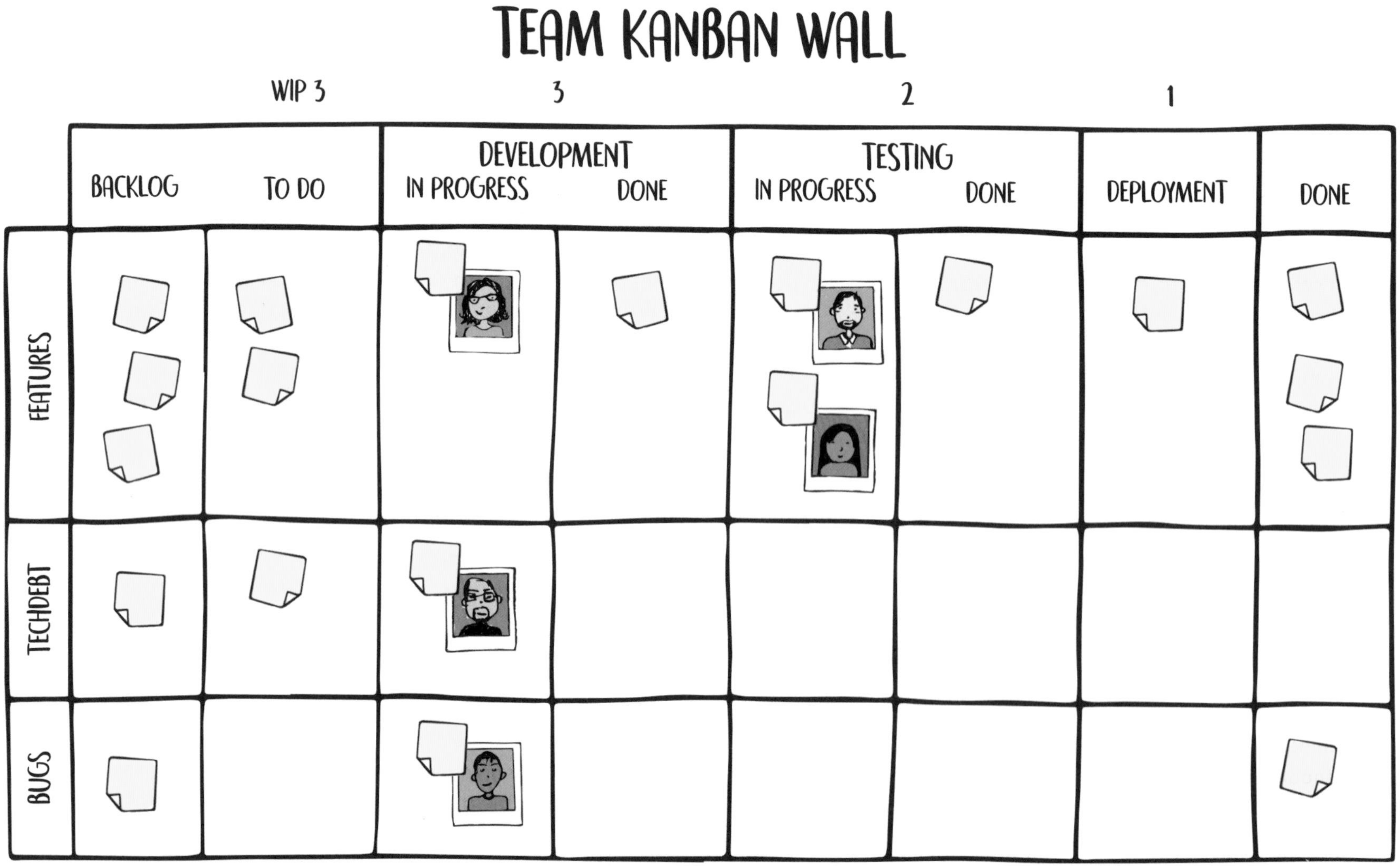
TEAM KANBAN WALL
WIP 3
3
2
1
BACKLOG
TO DO
DEVELOPMENT
IN PROGRESS
DONE
TESTING
IN PROGRESS
DONE
DEPLOYMENT
DONE
FEATURES
TECHDEBT
BUGS

some to bugs and tech debt. But it's still one card, one person. The principle is to break the work down much further than happens in Scrum, and to have that work breakdown as a visible picture of the overall resource allocation, cost, and schedule.

Yes, you could use Scrum. The cards become the backlog of work. But the fastest they will be delivered is a two- to three-week cycle (or Sprint). Sadly, Scrum is often nothing more than a mini-waterfall. That means no delivery for weeks, and then a deluge of features delivered in one go, which increases the risk of bugs, since some items in this deluge will overwrite others. Going back to the film analogy, we should remind ourselves we are filming by camera angle—the smallest piece of work we can imagine—rather than by scene.

Kanban eliminates many of the issues that arise from complexity because each feature is delivered as soon as it's complete and it's just one version. The software is never branched.

For the technical amongst you, there are many publications out there that go into this in more detail. For those of you who are non-technical, you are getting a glimpse of the religious wars of Scrum versus Kanban happening in IT departments around the world!

We should be more firm here. Throw away Scrum and use Kanban. **Flow** works best with this process.

The Team Kanban Wall shows work throughput (or cycle time). It even shows who is working on what and what is not being worked on at all. And tasks can be deprioritised or, alternatively, re-prioritised right up until the last moment.

Flow is also as much a project-accounting system as it is work process. The cards, or Post-it notes, each represent something that is in the act of being realised as well as the resources allocated to it.

A simple count of the cards, from the initial definition of the project to its final completion, reveals the best product managers and business analysts in your company, the ones who do good work breakdown, or not as the case may be. The knack for improving productivity is to make them role models.

THE CYCLE TIME ISSUE

Work breakdown is critical to **flow** because of the importance of cycle time. Cycle time refers to the length of time it takes to complete a typical software task. In Flow we are trying to get our cycle time down to one or two days – or even quicker!

In Agile environments cycle time can be as short as 20 days but as long as 80 to 100 days. Of course, in Agile, teams will have regular sprints in order to reach milestones as set out in the plan but very often the objective of sprints is to accelerate towards a goal that in Flow terms is just too large to be managed properly.

In order for software teams to be organised across a time span of anything from 20 - 100 days, they will be working on branches of code that might take slightly different directions and then need merging & integrating before being handed on to the operations team. The pressure will be on to deliver on time and that invariably means that important elements of testing will be overlooked. Integrating the work of different teams can be a struggle in itself, requiring a lot of rework or churn, particularly if one team is late.

The result is often that the code handed over by the development team is in a state that causes operational problems. In all of this, IT wraps itself in its own concerns and procedures and loses sight of the key goal - creating value for customers. For the good of the organisation and customers these issues need to be addressed.

With **flow**, it would appear that there is no branching. However, because of good work breakdown, the integrations happen so quickly that in fact the branching is irrelevant and the team experiences no code collisions. If an issue appears, it's much easier to back out of the work of a few hours rather than a few weeks or even months.

The analogy we used earlier is with making movies. This great creative act is in fact broken down into its smallest components before shooting begins. Why? Because every single professional on a movie set then understands what she has to do in relation to every other professional - makeup, photography, continuity, sound, lighting etc.

Making it work in practice
9. THE RECIPE FOR PROCESS CHANGE

There are areas of business that work exceptionally well by adopting one variation or another of the commissioning model. IT often stands in the way of this because it is so relentlessly technical in its language and so unforgiving in the detail it applies to process.

We believe that can be changed by thinking of pictures, Mosaics, and craft. To get this right still requires the discipline of breaking work down but heck, Disney movie animators do it so why can't we?

Choose language and metaphors relevant to your own company where appropriate. The changes we need to be aware of are:

■ Hierarchy becomes commissioning.

■ The business plan or project is a series of working hypotheses.

■ MVPs or prototypes are guided by development budgets.

■ All work becomes proof, evidence that value is close to hand.

■ Gamification comes into its own. (Why do you think there are so many awards ceremonies in TV and film? These guys like to win).

■ Visualisation becomes more and more important.

Another part of process redesign is to be programmatic about taking sacrosanct rituals in your organisation and disrupting them. For example, eschew the meeting room. (Fin used to have one but he turned it into a mini-sports stadium replete with fake grass.) In its place, start to take real pride in your Project Wall. This is where you are going to imagine the Mosaic and where you will break work down into segments that are meaningful and where costs are evident.

To do this successfully you need to include all the stakeholders to a project. If a project affects marketing, then the Mosaic has to be seen from marketing's perspective. It will help IT if they know how the marketer sees her role, especially if she goes into detail about what is necessary in order to fulfil her obligations. If it is inherently an IT issue, it will still need to be seen from the perspective of various users. Each of these has a role to play in creating the Project Wall.

A WORKING EXAMPLE OF *FLOW* FOR STRATEGY

SO FAR, WE HAVE TALKED
ABOUT A PRETTY WIDE
RANGE OF ISSUES. MANY
OF THEM MAY BE NEW TO
YOU SO WE WILL RECAP
BEFORE DIGGING INTO AN
EXAMPLE DRAWN FROM
STRATEGY. WHAT DID WE
TALK ABOUT OVER THE
LAST 160 PAGES OR SO?

1　The importance of **flow** in a highly scaled business where velocity is a key.

2　Ways of learning and the paramount importance of beliefs and social interaction.

3　Making the customer visible.

4　The three phases of culture (industrial, services, and **flow**).

5　Challenging the executive suite.

6　The overwhelming importance of pushing visualisation to extremes in order to provide a focal point for interaction and decision-making.

7　The sequencing of Walls.

8　The new qualities of leaders.

9　What a primary **flow** team should entail from Wall to Wall, Portfolio to Project to KanBan.

Now, we'll look at digital transformation and strategy through an example. In doing so, we will reiterate some of our thoughts about how to learn. But we are also going to talk about the next important skills and philosophies in **flow**:

■ The importance of **flow** in keeping delivery of value going and resisting the drift that big projects create.

■ The nature of social interaction as a complex learning system where everyone has a voice.

BREAKING BREAD WITH REALITY

Earlier we talked about the typical priorities of the executive suite. One frequently stated objective of top executives is "Put the customer front and centre". We also, somewhat facetiously, said that executive offsites continuously create new priorities by burying the ones from the previous year. Rather like a medieval city that gets submerged over time when you Walk the Wall and Bring Out the Dead, you find many priorities that deserved burying are still in circulation.

The importance of the customer, however, will be around for a long time to come. But it needs to be made operational in different parts of the business. Many new ideas are emerging around that. As we find customer experience inescapable, the large consultancies have inevitably moved in.

You may remember earlier we discussed **flow** in terms of the activity and knowledge that feeds into the

Executive Portfolio Wall, the place where priorities are translated into projects. Walls for strategy and culture are not fast changing and dynamic in the way that Project Walls are. Rather, they are a repository of what the company is learning.

Companies are launching digital transformation projects with no real sense of the before and after, nor of transformation as a work in progress. They expect a result like a single view of the customer when, in reality, what they need is a continuous dialogue about customers.

In this example, the company's objective is to get the customer front and centre. Doing so needs a critical transformation in how they use data. They want to launch one big customer-centric data project. The issue this raises for **flow** advocates is how to apply **flow** principles to big transformation projects. Our priority is to keep on adding value - in small discrete steps. But many big projects put value deep into the future, a strategy full of risk. Let's see how we can think about this differently. Think back to Chapter 5 where we dummied up this short list of executive's top five priorities:

■ Customer front and centre.

■ Going digital.

■ Offence: delivering upside through new

market entry; increased share of wallet.

■ Defence: cost focus / rationalisation.

■ Prioritising innovation and change

Now, the CEO of a fictional company has read about new techniques that give a single view of the customer and thinks this is great, so the "customer front and centre" priority gets restated as a technical one. The big priority becomes how to get a single view of the customer from all the data that the company hosts in its various servers. The priority is suddenly not the people or the customer. It is the technology of big data. We are, potentially, on our way to another tech-fest. Is technology the best way to get the customer front and centre? Maybe not, but we are about to make that idea a normative problem.

MY GREAT BIG FAT NORMATIVE PROJECT PROBLEM

We refer to the single view of the customer (SVOTC) as a normative problem because, like other choice phrases, it gets the same endorsement across many different industries. It quickly becomes the norm in conversations about innovation. That means many areas of work become normative whether they are true or not. It's a corner we keep painting ourselves into.

Consulting companies like IBM and Accenture are often the source of new business norms. They have great thought leadership but they also have a pressing need to keep finding work for highly paid consultants. They survive by codifying new platforms or technologies into business concepts that they can own and sell aggressively in order to put thousands of their people to work.

Conversely, in the face of the jargon deluge, companies struggle to discern what they really, truly need. Doubt and uncertainty are a consequence of being surrounded by very powerful vendor communities whose members devise new concepts and then successfully propagandise them into the market

The purpose of **flow** in this situation is to maintain a sense of proportion and to find ways to improve the company, even as decisions on big initiatives work their way through procurement. To take small steps towards value can be a sanity check, showing the executive team that the company can make progress without spending millions of dollars. Whether it can truly help resist the big vendor sales' machine is another question. **Flow** can at least keep the focus on the real objectives: continuous improvement in customer value.

The argument for SVOTC, the one that sets up the big project, goes something like this:

"We need a single view of the customer, an investment aimed at producing far better opportunities to upsell and cross-sell as we mine data effecively."

Concepts like SVOTC are simplifications of complex organisational change tasks. They carry a huge amount of baggage with them, not least that most companies have no idea what data they have or how to make it usable. Implicit in the above statement, then, is the expectation that getting a single view of the customer will take some years and many millions of dollars.

Other issues that lurk in the background include:

Vendor push

We already mentioned that these concepts are designed by vendors, such as consulting firms and tech platform firms, which means there is a huge marketing push behind them that is difficult for executives to resist. The concepts very quickly take on the character of "must have or be left behind." In our experience, many SVOTC platforms fail because they are implemented too quickly and with inadequate process redesign.

Big Projects

These are huge disruptions and come with enormous requirements because they involve introducing new platforms that need a large measure of integration. Most organisations will have multiple platforms where user data is kept, and most will not know what data they keep. On top of that, the different platforms will not talk to each other, and so creating a SVOTC from this is quite a challenge. Many CIOs want to move away from these big projects but they can become irresistible because the pitch is made to the CEO.

Silo conflict

Multiple different silos in an organisation create a sense of ownership and competition over the project and its outcomes. Some of the data might "belong" to marketing, while the CIO may think his department owns the technology. The chief data scientist, meanwhile, may think the entire project is hers. All want kudos from a good outcome and want to avoid odour from a bad one. All of this creates negative competition and places constraints on collaboration.

High preparatory costs

Very often, SVOTC projects require some kind of data-normalisation process and the creation of some kind of reference-data layer, neither of which is trivial. In AI, data normalisation can be 90 percent of the cost of a project.

These are all difficult problems to deal with. However there is an upside to the discussion around this, even if SVOTC is not achieved. SVOTC represents an opportunity to move technology and data to the cloud, introducing the ability to reduce cost and increase the pace of innovation. It presents an opportunity to simplify and future-proof the technology base but that is our gain not the customers.

THE FLOW-THINKING RESCUE DIET

Most organisations become normative in their thinking or veer towards a general consensus that sends damaging vibes down from the C-Suite. The **flow** solution is different. We think how can we protect our mission of continuously improving how we create value. OK, we don't want to duck SVOTC but nor do we want to be overrun by it. Big projects create big gaps in value creation. We've seen these big projects once too often.

At their very mention, alarm bells will be ringing for anyone over 25 years of age.

In **flow**, our priority is customer value and it does not take a genius to see that SVOTC is an investment that will benefit us, the company, without any clear reference point for how it will benefit the customer. The real answer of course is that customers get to buy more of our products or services. So how does that benefit them? It's a matter of integrity that we find out.

In **flow**, as well as asking the customer's questions, we also focus on the short-term gains. Just a step or two at a time that will help us to learn more about this new SVOTC challenge and add value as we take the first steps towards it.

SVOTC is part of the larger creative challenge of understanding how to function as a digital business, how to transform, and how that helps build customer satisfaction and long-term, loyal relationships.

Imagine, then, a section of the Customer Wall devoted to SVOTC. The concept can be broken into three areas (or more, if you wish):

1 **Semantics:** What do we really mean by this term?

2 **Resources:** What will be the overall cost?

3 **Vision:** How does it fit with or alter our vision?

1 Semantics

This should come first, so we can figure out what SVOTC actually means.

Take a few index cards and gather a few colleagues around. SVOTC means:

- A data-driven method of cross-selling or upselling to customers.

- Potentially a lower cost of sale and therefore a higher margin.

- An opportunity to segment the market in new ways through data.

- The potential for customer loyalty but also the potential to create problems around privacy.

- Potentially transitioning away from advertising and mass marketing to what's becoming known as "the market of one" (i.e., getting enough data to sell at scale to each individual).

- Potentially buying a vendor platform or solution, even if we may not need one. Creating an imbalance in departmental budgets.

- Probably an opportunity to extend data-capture to the customer call centres, which will anyway be buying bots to automate customer transactions and build new data sources.

- An opportunity to move infrastructure to the cloud and retire some legacy technology.

Those are the kinds of implications of SVOTC. Those cards can hang there on the Wall for a while.

2 Resources

SVOTC is going to suck resources from all over the organisation if it is allowed to proceed as a normative project. Other projects will become constrained as a result and SVOTC will likely become the primary focus of digital transformation (as it has for many marketing-led companies).

3 Vision

What is the ultimate gain from any given project? Ultimately, the vision needs to be a better outcome for the customer at an acceptable cost to the organisation.

Some companies have now racked up appalling damage to their customer relationships through upselling and cross-selling, particularly those in financial services (who have also faced heavy fines

for inappropriate selling). That's why, from a **flow** perspective, it pays to be cautious and ask what the customer really gains from a project and how value can be delivered quickly.

In many industries, services or products are designed to lack value in order to push the upsell (products like the BMW 1 series and the seating in economy class aircraft are designed to push aspiring people to the next level, the BMW 3, 4, 5, 6, or 7, or business-class tickets, respectively).

Now, we're not out to change the practices of a whole industry, but we can refresh the vision.

The vision is of a company that continues to add value to the customer's experience of a product, perhaps through daily changes to its capabilities, which in turn adds value to the customer's life.

What is different about this perspective is that it refrains from building the business around forcing the upsell. Most car companies, for example, struggle to manage their credit portfolios because their dealerships have effectively sold financial stress to their clients. Businesses are full of costs created by such bad selling strategies.

Ask yourself, "Should my company really spend

millions on a brute-force system to sell more to customers that they might find irrelevant or might not really want or can't afford?".

Either way, you have to be very careful about the changes you implement and how you communicate those changes. For example, in some parts of the world, there is a distinct and growing wariness of corporate-data usage, to the point where the acronym B2B is being replaced by ME2B to indicate customer control of data in the relationship. As we wander into SVOTC, data issues like that lie in wait.

On the other hand, many of us need to upgrade legacy IT and preferably migrate to the cloud to keep up with new customer demands around scale, scope, and speed. Those facts make data an essential part of the customer-business relationship.

These conflicting thoughts need to find their way onto the Digital Business Wall, where we are trying to redefine the fundamentals of the business. We need many eyes focused on that challenge, so the questions need to be out in the open.

We need to create a wall that gives us an opportunity to explore issues more broadly and to explore other perspectives on customer value. As always, we create the relevant columns. In this case they can be seen on page 181: Technologies, Ethnography, Engagement, and Other. We need to complement the Digital Business Wall with more Issues. This would include a view of any downstream consequences of SVOTC. The cards don't have to carry very complex messages or be formally written. The simpler the statements the better, especially when it comes to assessing risk:

- Cross-selling, upselling: Which products? Appropriate selling or inappropriate? Risk to reputation?

- Which existing projects can we choke back without losing value?

- What talent does a migration to SVOTC need and where will it come from?

- ME2B Movement, reverse data: Is SVOTC the right long-term bet?

- New platform to consolidate existing data? Cloud is good. Data normalisation and better reference data could contribute.

- Big vendor implementation? Risk to company culture?

- Cloud migration: opportunities to further microservices' architecture? Cost savings?

Issues like these must become the focal point of

discussion. Over the course of the social interaction around them, a simple step forward will emerge, along with a moral position.

Why moral? Well, you are committed to enhancing customer value. At the same time, many businesses wish to maximise revenue at all times. These are not always compatible goals. The right call for the long term is to side with the customer but that position will come under pressure from others in the organisation. Within the constraints of a corporate consensus mechanism, you have to stand up for what the organisation says it believes in. Is it the customer or is it the upsell?

In thinking about these issues, you want to push for new insights into your relationship with customers, and the biggest one is staring you in the face.

How about instead of a single view *of* the customer we think in terms of a single view *for* the customer.

This is in line with the vision of improving the customer's life at an acceptable cost. It also suggests a course of action, one so simple it eludes many companies:

Let's talk to customers.

In place of embarking on the implementation of a multimillion-dollar platform, let's first invite customers in and talk to them.

Introducing the customer to the development dialogue is actually an imperative, certainly in **flow**, but actually in every business.

"Where I work now," say Fin, *"we already host a lot of school parties that come into our offices. We sponsor IT equipment in some of the less wealthy Dublin suburbs and we have the kids in to play around with the apps we are creating. It's already very instructive for us. But what we really want is a customer lab, where the conversations become more frequent."*

Technologies like big data and AI have made huge differences in the way we do business but they will never be substitutes for the natural human interaction between you and the people who buy your products and services.

Taking the above into consideration, your *Single View FOR the Customer* (SVFTC) project now starts to look like this:

1 **Creating a customer venue:** Resource a customer lab and customer dialogue venues in the building, at places where customers

gather, or even at a pop up in a nearby town. The cost is minimal and the benefit is that you get feedback on all existing products and pipeline plans. All this will only help creativity. You'll also get a new voice in the pipeline—the voice of the customer—that will find its way onto the Walls.

2 **New market segmentation:** As an interim step, while the new platform is under development, you can draw up a new set of market segments as described in chapter 1. Those new segments go up on the Wall, and the team comes up with new ways to adapt the **flow** and serve more micro-segments.

3 **Customer loyalty:** Depending on how much you invest in the dialogue with customers, you become an advocate for them rather than just a sniper out to hit a target. Smart marketers will use this to reach the broader customer community and enhance the sense of unity between company and customer.

4 **Resources:** You still have to make decisions on resources but it is worth thinking about what that means in this new context. You want to resource customer interaction, which can be done by choking back a project or two.

5 **Vision:** It is in place and enriched. You are more visibly committed to the customer.

Now, you need to consider what will make your SVFTC different from everybody else's. A new conversation begins. Other companies all around you are doing SVOTC but you have flipped it round.

Cards start to go up on the Wall:

- What would this industry look like in 2, 5, and 10 years' time if... ME2B gets momentum?

- We really could personalise to markets of one if we embrace ME2B.

- How does AI play into a SVFTC and ME2B?

- How to realise significant gains from a single view for the customer within two years?

Having people who can start these conversations makes for a more exciting workplace. Suddenly, we're no longer in an old-fashioned organisation dominated by vendor aggression and people who push company policy around like a steam roller, dampening enthusiasm in the process.

Making it work in practice

10. A WALL FOR RECONFIGURING DIGITAL STRATEGY

In this section, we are going to transpose the thinking from the past few pages into a Wall exercise that challenges corporate strategy in a fundamental way.

The underlying principles are the same as those in the last section but we will apply it to one industry—automobiles—to make it more concrete.

In this example, a mandate comes down from the C-Suite to create a SVOTC. The CEO has seen a news report that a competitor is working on one, and he's been sold heavily at his club by the CEO of a vendor company. Not having a SVOTC currently is affecting his golf swing.

People start to scramble around looking for how SVOTC works. The first reaction is to talk with vendors. But this is a holistic company with a good Wall process and a desire for visual and transparent work processes.

There is a further point to consider. We are in the platform age. Companies that achieve durable competitive success will tend to have a platform strategy. Think Facebook, a platform for sharing personal content and (supposedly) contextual advertising. Apple is a platform for apps, content, and mobile-phone utility. Alibaba is a platform for global trade.

In the automotive industry, there is a realistic expectation that cars are becoming a kind of platform. This will only increase once autonomous vehicles are commonplace. For hours a day, auto companies will hold people captive to screens on the dashboard and/or the smartphone. Undoubtedly, there will be scope to grow a content and developer ecosystem but in competition with Google, Netflix, Facebook, etc.

Right now, however, most automakers have poor platform strategies. Their profitable revenue streams do not lie in car sales. Rather, the cash cow is after-sales service and extra parts. And to capitalise on this, they need extremely good customer retention. Retention issues are critcal to profitability.

As long as a car's service warranty is in place the dealer can incentivise loyalty: if customers do not have their cars serviced at a dealer's garage, the warranty is void. After the service warranty expires, however, customer loyalty drops off a cliff as people go in search of cheaper servicing or no servicing at all.

This is the backdrop for the CEO's call for a SVOTC. The CEO's strategic position is that he needs to transform to a platform company but in the meantime he has to sustain and hopefully increase his parts' revenues. He wants to know exactly how he can leverage the behavioural profiles that SVOTC offers in order to incentivise people back into the dealerships after the end of a service warranty.

Here's how we might develop the initial Wall to address the issue of customer retention and platform strategy.

In a non-**flow** context, the work would be broken down as per the column on the left. There would be some feasibility work around the technology, and it would include data discovery (e.g., What data do we actually collect?) as well as what that means in terms of having to normalise data, construct reference data and master data management around it. And there would have to be some workflow discovery around how the new project will change work processes.

Each of these is a substantial project in its own right and needs the detail articulated. And each fits into different strategic flows such as the one that goes into and out of the long term goal of digital transformation.

The problem that this car company faces is not actually SVOTC or its technical requirements, though it can quickly appear as though the technical challenges are an end in themselves.

The problem for automakers is customer retention. That's what we really need to address. So it pays to step back and remind ourselves of this. What problem are we really addressing?

We have sketched in some time horizons on the

Wall, too. You can see that most elements of a SVOTC project are in excess of twelve months, and they are XL in size. A far-sighted CTO will see the dangers of her company getting swamped by this project. She will look to other tools and smaller steps than these, without losing sight of the fact that some form of big data or AI project is inevitable. It's a way to go but to do it right now, straight out of the blocks, is going to squeeze out too many other options.

In posting the problem to the Wall, the CTO has invited a holistic view of how customer insights can be acquired, with particular emphasis on this being an exercise to further our knowledge of the customer rather than just being about a technical implementation.

One column, headed Ethnography, poses the question: Can we study customers in some shorter time horizon than the SVOTC platform to create new data about their needs?

The next is Engagement. Are there customer engagement tools that will help us go further along the path?

And finally, the is a column called Other. This signals a desire to expose other useful tools to the team.

An ethnographic project could be quick—less than three months. The same applies to Engagement.

These kinds of projects are also easy to commission. The CTO asks for a staff member with a background in

PLATFORM STRATEGY AND CUSTOMER RETENTION EVALUATION

PROJECT	TECH SOLUTION	SIZE	HORIZON	ETHNOGRAPHY	SIZE	HORIZON	ENGAGE	SIZE	HORIZON	OTHER	SIZE	HORIZON
	FEASIBILITY	XL	12	DEALER PROFILE	S	3	LAB	S	3	SEGMENT	S	3
	DATA DISCOVERY	L	9							ME2B	S	3
	DATA NORM	XL	12									
	WORKFLOW DISCOVERY	M	6									
	VENDER RFP	S	9									

sociology to spend time in dealerships, and she sets up a small welcome room in a town pop-up shop to have her people just talk to customers and engage them with the company's challenges.

Meanwhile, she also decides to commission a proof of concept (PoC) of a SVOTC solution.

The illustration on the previous page shows the results of these steps with the possibility of a T-shirt size being allocated to the issues identified.

While the PoC is being figured out, some new thoughts have gone up in the "Other" column, and the ethnography and engagement teams report back.

From the ethnography we find that:

1   In most cases, customer issues are LARGE.

2   There are serious gender issues in many dealerships, particularly when women arrive to hand over their car keys and then later when picking up a serviced car. The environment of the garage is just too male oriented and outdated. Beyond the garage, the sales personnel tend to be men and the reception is managed by a woman. It looks like 1980. As well, it makes no concession to the fact that some of the customers have children with them and need to get them to school, kindergarten, etc.

3   The dealer lot is empty for most of the time. Apart from Saturdays, the cars stand like gleaming monuments of a past age, and the only people looking at them are the sales staff.

4   Selling is aggressive and subtly gladiatorial, with an implicit emphasis on shaming customers into the upsell (**Can't afford it buddy, huh?**). This makes customers visibly uncomfortable and risks straining the company's credit portfolio as people are persuaded to buy cars they cannot afford.

5   There is inflexible scheduling for servicing cars, meaning many customers need to arrange a lift from the garage to the workplace (having already taken an hour off work for the drop-off). Or they have to walk to work or push a pram down the forecourt to get home. Same at pick up time. No wonder they don't want to come back.

6 The initial engagement research reinforces that conclusion. Lifts, or a lack of them, are a major reason why people don't go to the dealership service.

7 A school visit shows that next to no girls envision themselves as mechanics, though they are interested in the allure of cars.

8 The "Other" column reveals a major drift against the use of customer data for sales, inspired by companies like SNAP and their disappearing photo service.

9 In addition, there is more regulatory pressure coming on data usage that may compromise vendor solutions.

10 The new customer segmentation tells you that a significant portion of the customer base is actually quite interested in cycling and the outdoors. But this is only one segment among many that give clues as to how a platform could help them more. (Sell bike parts? Partner with other mobility solutions? Provide AR-mapping apps for customer outings?) Ironically, the fans of the car company are different from those of the services and parts division. Servicing attracts a much more aspirational customer segment (see page 185) and people with a deeper interest in cars.

11 Finally, this new ME2B movement promises to shape data storage in ways customers can control. Facebook has backed it and Apple has been making similar noises. It is going to have an impact on corporate data use.

All this information is in before the SVOTC project enters its PoC. What it tells you is that:

■ The technical solution is long term, complex, and will be subject to pressures that have not been anticipated by vendors of the SVOTC solution. The lack of opportunity for short-term value creation poses the risk of a big project eating up resources and creating delivery risk.

■ There is a strong need to anticipate pivot points in the tech project, which needs to sit within a single view **for** the customer. Nonetheless, the PoC will undoubtedly show that the SVOTC project should go ahead—tech vendors are very persuasive.

- A program of customer retention can be launched alongside the SVOTC project. The SVOTC needs to be within a flow of information about changing attitudes and regulatory requirements.

- The platform strategy should seek better ways of using real estate. It should find better ways to schedule customer appointments and assist with onward journeys; have an outreach element to sell cars in different locations; consider gender balance (offering female mechanic apprenticeships); look at third-party assets that can pass through the dealership by taking the customer segmentation to heart; probably migrating them to multimodal opportunites at dealerships; create marketing programmes that convert the petrolhead customer to somebody with an appreciation of the broader culture of the auto and its future.

These aspects of customer knowledge need to inform the overall project. The dream of having a data source that can flick a switch in customers' heads and make them more likely to buy or return for services is just that—a dream.

The SVFTC suggests a much more holistic solution to the problem. The lessons can now be framed as SVFTC projects and be streamed into the **flow**, starting with evaluation.

CUSTOMER INSIGHT WALL

INTERESTS	AUTOS	BRANDS	PEOPLE	POST-SALES SERVICE
MARKETING	PERFORMANCE CARS	FORD	BILL GATES	MORE BMW
TECHNOLOGY	OFF ROAD	YOUTUBE	PAULO COELHO	MORE MERCEDES
TRAVEL	RACING	CHEVROLET	JEREMY CLARKSON	HUMOUR
PERSONAL FINANCE	MOTORCYCLES	HARLEY	DANIEL TOSH	VINTAGE CARS (MUCH MORE)
SCIENCE AND TECHNOLOGY	VINTAGE	INSTAGRAM	CHRIS ANDERSON	BUSINESS
		TWITTER		WINE
				RADIO

WORK AS A LEARNING MODEL

THE ACADEMY

We began this book with a small number of simple hypotheses:

- *"Good decisions stem from good social interaction."*

- *"Learning arises from social interaction more than it does from the transfer of information from one person to another or through creativity."*

- *"Belief is the single biggest responsibility of a leader."*

- *"Nurturing belief in others is a burden that few leaders accept."*

We have also pointed to research that shows how *"share of conversation"* among members of teams is a critical factor in creating good work.

What all of these factors have in common is that they are intensely personal. And therein lies the rub for conventional management and leadership techniques. There is no hierarchy, performance review, or silo where people can hide from the power of relationships.

Instead, the organisation depends on leaders who know how to shape conversations and those who are able to sustain themselves under conditions of uncertainty.

No change program will deliver these assets. If you want them, you have to create the learning environment.

In this final chapter, we will address learning head on. As mentioned earlier, learning has four elements: **Creativity**, **Learning Transfer**, **Belief** and **Social Interaction**

We will talk about learning in the context of what we call The Academy Wall, or just The Academy. Yes, the term is a little portentous but it captures the range of learning activities that good social interaction facilitates. An Academy sounds about right, at least if we refuse to take ourselves too seriously.

To recap on learning:

Creativity

This is the long-term reinvention of processes. It is far too easy to see creativity in short-term gains like a new app, feature or service. But when you look across industries, creativity is all about how organisations reinvent themselves over lengthy periods of time. It is an unimaginably complex process. The best example remains Apple, who from 2000 to 2012 put right a lot of its past failures and transformed in a variety of ways. That process also involves individuals in reimagining their own roles and skills.

In organisational terms, this is the meaning of creativity, the capacity to take the whole organisation through successive major transformations in order to reinvent it. And in these companies, management has the stomach for big bets backed by big belief.

Learning Transfer

Companies try, over and over, to transfer information by passing knowledge from one person to another: from a conference speaker to an audience, from a workshop leader to a team, from a manager to a newbie. This has proven difficult for both sides because people work within rules laid down by big software systems. It has become problematic now that we are liberating ourselves from Big Software.

Belief

Many of the barriers to learning exist because people have deep, core frameworks that inform their day-to-day activities. It has taken parenting, schooling, and community life to create those frameworks, and they are not really fungible. Psychologist Stellan Ohlsson tells us we need to frame new experiences within people's existing core frameworks if we are to succeed in changing their behaviour.

How that might happen, efficiently, is really a matter of guesswork or intuition. Dan Pontefract, who leads transformation at Telus, Canada's largest mobile network, believes there is a key paradox in the transition from childhood and school to work.

For the most part, we are brought up to believe we must think for ourselves. In principle, the journey from adolescence to adulthood is a transition away from dependencies (on parents, schools, etc.) to an independent mindset. But the organisations we then go to work for deny us access to this hard-earned asset. At work, for the past fifty years, there has been little scope for independent minds.

There is an element of inevitability about that. Organisations need loyalty and can't find space for a great deal of maverick behaviour. But how they go about securing that loyalty and conformity strikes against the instincts of many free-thinking people: the insistence on alignment with bad plans, processes that bore people into depressive moods, and the political contest for advancement.

We said earlier that you need to work with employee's belief in the right to think freely. In an era where people spend more time concerned with work and less with their personal lives, they have the right to believe leaders will care about this.

Social interaction

Finally, we have sung the virtues of good interaction and setting the scene for it, visually. The evidence shows that when more people in a team get a chance to speak, project outcomes are better. Full stop. And the evidence shows that visible lessons are more easy to grasp.

But there is so much more to the idea of social interaction than that.

The way we think, form opinions, and assimilate information today is different from what it was two decades ago. We have very little time, opportunity, or inclination for reflection. And yet we have to think, reflect, and absorb, from a constant and abundant **flow** of information.

The new philosophy of how we think, of cognition, more or less accepts that we function through what can be termed "neural, bodily, and environmental processes"[11].

Pierre Levy has raised the possibility that the most fundamental change is not just in the environmental tools that help us think (from pen and paper to computer and internet) but in the enormous flow of information that we must somehow shape to our advantage.

It stands to reason that shaping the flow has to be done through social interaction and visualisation. Why?

Just as we need a pen and paper to do some kinds of maths, and humble Scrabble pieces to come up with words in a game, we need some form of external tooling to help us think about information flows.

The critical information flows for work can be:

- New techniques from vendors, open source, meetups, etc.

- The experiences of others in our milieu.

- Third-party data on the resegmentation of markets or changes in customer needs.

- Internal data from data warehouses.

- Trial and error.

- System-performance metrics.

- Personal capabilities.

- Emotional entanglements or disturbances in people's lives.

- Resource availability (even to the simple degree of knowing who is on sick leave or when vacations arise).

- System redesigns.

Social interaction and the right visual representations of knowledge allow many eyes to view and review the knowledge flow. They allow people to see the overall Script of a company's progress and to collaborate in real-time with their colleagues. Collective intelligence becomes social intelligence, which means the group is making the many additional decisions firms now require.

But all of this needs multiple forms of support. To date, we have looked at visualisations. The idea of The Academy means more than that. Primarily, the additional factor lies in finding the right story formats for learning.

11

"The Extended Mind"
Andy Clark and
David Chalmers

THE IDEA OF THE ACADEMY

The Academy has the same physical presence as everything else we have discussed: a Wall and people who talk. It includes:

The learning model

First of all, no tools invalidate the idea that social interaction is the primary channel for all learning. Rather, tools are ways to help inform and shape the conversations that take place.

The learning model is a mix of interaction and additional targeted activities. It includes set times during the week to focus on learning, a kind of academy time where strands of new experience can be documented on the Learning Wall.

Academy time, which should be treated as an event, should be happening once a week, even if just for a half hour.

This idea of meeting to learn is sometimes referred to as a "retrospective" in Agile. However, problems can arise with retrospectives:

- They are always backwards looking.

- They tend to point the finger at people and can be uncomfortable, scapegoating experiences rather than valued didactic ones.

- They do not draw in external experiences such as new learning from outside the organisation.

- They happen at the end of projects, when the problems have already exacted a price.

The Academy is a more comprehensive learning experience and is meant to challenge the place of retrospectives. It is a better way to learn.

At the top of the diagram on the next page, you can see some of the tools we will discuss in this chapter.

On the right, external experiences, such as engagement with the open-source community or meetups, conferences, and jams, are brought into the learning event (they can be posted to the Learning Wall so that people get a preview).

At the bottom of the diagram, you see more formal news sources. For example, if you work with the consultancy ThoughtWorks, you will have access to their Technology Radar. If not, you will be reading websites like TheNextWeb or following sites like Linux Foundation.

On the left, there are project-course-correction documents or experiences. What has been learned

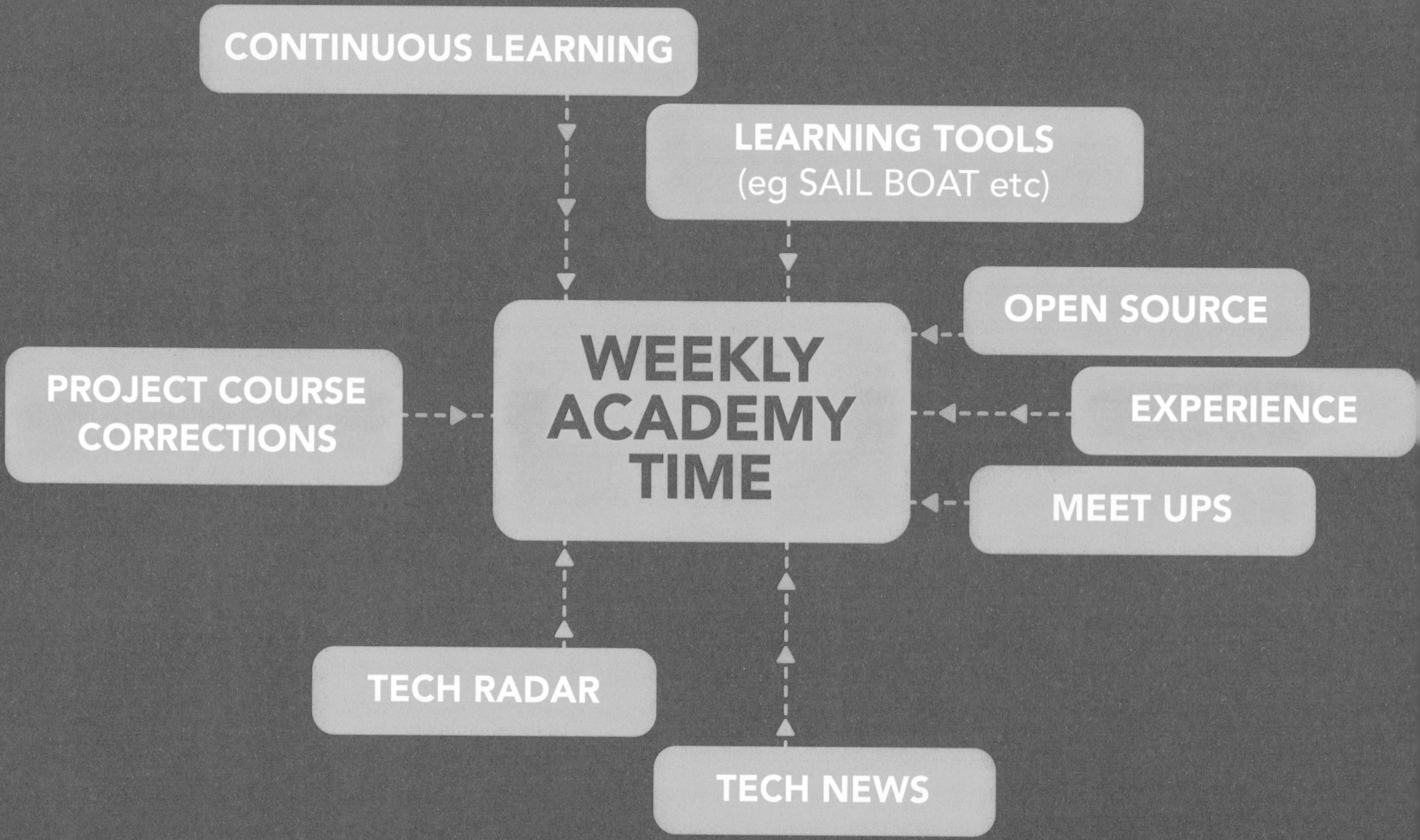
CONTINUOUS LEARNING
LEARNING TOOLS
(eg SAIL BOAT etc)
OPEN SOURCE
PROJECT COURSE CORRECTIONS
WEEKLY ACADEMY TIME
EXPERIENCE
MEET UPS
TECH RADAR
TECH NEWS

from other parts of the project or other projects in the company this week?

These can be brought in as topical reminders that good practices are being built all the time and that some problems have already been solved elsewhere in the team.

The Learning Wall

The Learning Wall is the repository for every new piece of information that people want to share. Like all Walls, it is a space to pin up short summaries, not essays. Organise the Wall in your own way but perhaps start with the diagram above. Those four elements should suffice.

Take a card and summarise, in a sentence, what was learned from tackling a new problem, deciding to abandon a piece of work, taking on a new tool, or accelerating a novel solution. What is new in the Customer Lab or Wall, what's being learned from meetups? Just one card, one sentence.

Technology Radar

You need access to information on new techniques, tools, platforms, and frameworks. But having access to information is easy. The hard part is using it as a key asset among teams. As far as possible, you want to understand people's experiences with new tools and techniques, and you need to figure out what to do with this information.

You may think this Tech Radar is irrelevant to the CFO or CMO. Yet most CFOs, in even smallish companies, now deal with multiple exotic currencies and need to find technologies that give them end-to-end control of cash. Most marketers are inundated with new ways to succeed on Pinterest, Instagram, Facebook, Google Plus, LinkedIn, SnapChat, and so on. They need a Tech Radar, and they need collective intelligence to shape technical information, just as much as the CIO and CTO do.

You can divide the task of evaluating tools into **Assess**, **Trial**, **Hold** and **Adopt**.

Those four elements are valid also for existing techniques. There should be a regular attempt at assessing the new tools used by staff, especially in shadow IT projects, trials of new tools, decisions to hold or discard existing tools, and decisions to adopt new ones.

If you don't have access to a third party radar, create your own. Keep in mind, though, that there is far too much out there for your department to track.

Tools like the tech radar are important for more than just giving valuable new information. Most developers will constantly be trying out new tools anyway. Marketers play with social media in their personal lives and come to work hyping up the next influencer, tool, or persona-building technique.

The problem is that staff may be adopting these ideas even if the tools are not the best way to get work done. The Cool Wall is meant to address that.

Cool Walls

The Cool Wall, you might remember us saying earlier (in Chapter 6), is the place where people can post their one liners about new techniques. It might sound frivolous to call it a one liner but we live in the world of Twitter, where @POTUS runs the world's largest economy through tweets. Being brief is powerful

We take those one-line suggestions and make them the topic for a serious Friday rundown on how we could do better. In Fin's case, he gets his teams to vote on which ideas need more elaboration and discussion before being adopted. That could be cool code for integrating video into a web page or great results in customer segmentation with StatSocial analysis, for example.

You should make a stipulation about inclusion. People are encouraged to try out new ways to work but they need to demonstrate the value or post the lack of value in public.

The Cool Wall needs these four categories:

This is a way to get ideas into the more formal **Assess**, **Trial**, **Hold**, **Adopt** process that we mentioned above.

The Friday Story

In one of Fin's departments, Friday afternoons are for storytelling. They are particularly reserved for stories about experiments and tests that people are doing (see The Cool Wall above). These are not retrospectives. They are perspectives on the future, on what can change for the better.

Storytelling involves both the business side and the IT side of the house. The objective is to have four or five people do five-minute pitches on what they are learning. These pitches could be about customers, tools, or solutions. The room should be full. We're talking 100 people or more (or for a smaller company, everybody) before they go off for the weekend. It is not a demo (as in Agile). It is a debate, an intellectual setting where the fit between how we understand customers and how we understand techniques gets aired and tested in public. These are also hypotheses about bringing the future into view.

Blue Ocean

In Blue Ocean thinking, based on the book **Blue Ocean Strategy**, about seeking out uncontested space in markets, there is a very simple approach to work. We adopt this approach to weekly review meetings.

It starts with what were we doing that we decided to kill off (because it didn't work). What new things are we doing that we are happy to continue with? Now that we have cleared some clutter from Stop Doing, what new things do we have the bandwidth to get started on?

The idea of the weekly Academy time is to focus on projects, their problems, and the solutions we are trying out. If you have the Cool Wall, Tech Radar and The Friday Story nailed down (or rather, tacked up on the Learning Wall), you are in a position to make judgments about what to stop, continue, or start.

The objective of the Blue Ocean segment of the Learning Wall is to identify a manageable amount of learning by bringing together the collective intelligence of the group.

Ask people to vote on the top three items in each of these columns (Stop, Continue, Start). Those columns, remember, consist of things people in your teams have been trying out. You are not seeking to embarrass anyone here. You are bringing a collective voice to decide what is and is not valid.

Sail Boat

Sail Boat is a friendly retrospective technique and a much kinder way to learn. Here's how to do Sail Boat.

You draw one big picture which includes a **Sail Boat**, an **Island**, **Wind in the Sails**, **Iceberg**, **Anchors**, **Clouds** and **Sharks**!

- The Island represents the teams goals and vision for the project and what we need to do in order to get a project back on course.

- The Wind in the Sails are the things that worked well and drove us forward.

- The Iceberg represents the risks and blockers that we encountered, which stopped us from achieving the goals and vision.

- The Anchors on the Sail Boat represent everything that slowed us down.

- The Clouds represent everything that worked well and the things that could help us in the future.

- And finally the Sharks. These are things that worked against us. Perhaps an executive who kept stealing team members - feel free to improvise.

Fin says, *"I attended a retro workshop recently and the facilitator used pirates to depict the audit team! A tad unfair, I hear you say... but the auditors loved it!*

Anyway, everyone in the session takes it in turns to write on Post-it notes the items that they believe fit into each category and then stick them on the picture. While we prefer one big picture it can get out of hand if there are too many people in the mix! If the group of people in retro is too large, then one can use individual flipcharts with each topic on one page. This does make it easier if there are lots of Post-it notes.

The facilitator looks for common points and removes duplicates. Multiple 'common' Post-it's are grouped together for a detailed discussion and very soon the key issues, blockers and things that propelled the team, come to the fore.

Some teams prefer to document the retro for wider distribution. It's quite easy to use PowerPoint or KeyNote to put one topic on each slide in order to pull out the key learnings.

But the reason that we prefer the one picture is that it can be placed on a wall near the team and serve not only as a reminder but also a visual representation for everyone in the company to see, use and learn.

And finally, do make sure that you re-iterate the Retrospective Prime Directive before any type of reflective process. Which is:

"Regardless of what we discover, we understand and truly believe that everyone did the best job they could, given what they knew at the time, their skills and abilities, the resources available, and the situation at hand".

Write it on a flip chart, hang it on the wall, use it as a positive affirmation of the process and you won't go wrong."

Metrics

Before going on to what could also be called lay-planning tools, we want to emphasise once more that the two metrics in constant use are:

1 **Value for the customer:** What are we providing for them and how closely can that be visualised and measured? Is the feature, function, or message important enough to impact satisfaction or uptake? The only way to find out is to talk with customers and deliver options they can try out.

2 **Cycle time:** By cycle time we mean the time

it takes to complete any single work package. If cycle time is decreasing, all is golden, or should be. It means you are faster at creating value. If it is increasing, then something is wrong. The source of the problem could be in work design. It could be in areas like sick leave or holidays. Or it could be that a team member is not capable of fulfilling the tasks assigned. But cycle time tells you it is one of these. If cycle time increases go unchecked, you are storing up resource issues.

Horizon Planning

Finally, we have emphasised throughout this book that planning happens through interaction.

That's not to say there are no formal techniques. Facebook, for example, uses a simple tool called Horizon Planning. There are plenty of ideas about the general concept of horizon planning but Facebook's is admirably simple and therefore usable.

Left to their own devices, leaders typically create impossible plans. They don't know enough about what's possible and what's changing, so they cannot plan ahead realistically. It is risible to fake omniscience in today's information flow. If leaders pretend they know everything, the folks around them are probably not going to follow.

So what are the good alternatives to yesterday's big plans? Some kind of conversational process is needed. It is simply about making a call on a three-, six-, nine-, or twelve-month horizon. That timescale is about right if the priority is to get things done without falling over and looking stupid.

Because leaders are typically out of touch, they need to socialise the question of what can be done on these timescales.

Take a look back at the Executive Portfolio Wall, examining the tasks that should deliver the C-Suite's objectives. Which can credibly be done within three months?

It is surprising how much the answer to that will vary across a team of people. But pose it at a planning standup. There will be folks there who know exactly how to crack the problem you have articulated and will tell you it fits squarely within a three-month timescale. Contrariwise, you will be posing three-month tasks that some people will tell you need pushing out to six or nine months.

You can do this planning exercise on a Wall too. We haven't tried it yet but why not go for it. Introduce a Horizon Wall.

Making it work in practice
11. THE RECIPE FOR HAPPY SAILING

In the City of Lyon, France, they have a dish called Fromage du Tête. It must be some kind of cheese, right? Well, sadly it is a vegetarian's worst nightmare. It consists of offal from a pig's head, all made up into what looks like a reasonably appetising pâté.

We mention Fromage du Tête simply to point out that things (events, processes, etc.) are often not what they seem.

People in organisations tend to want documentation, plans, proofs. What these really amount to is a demand for evidence that something is going to work. Or, to put it even more simply, evidence that the future is good and will arrive on time.

Asking for evidence is perfectly natural and a good demand to make. It may seem that what we have said to date in this book is a counter to that very good notion. It isn't. What we are saying, though, is that much of the documentation, plans, and proofs that get passed around organisations are often attempts to cover up for a lack of evidence or a bad plan. They have little practical value. They are Fromage du Tête.

Flow is real, shouldered by people who will care more about you, your leadership, and your products if you follow its principles.

We know many readers will be thinking, "Heck, you are so right. I never thought of it that way (:-))".

Seriously though, the big issue you might face is how to get going with **flow**. Where do you start?

Earlier on in the book, we pointed out that customer segmentation, understanding the market in new ways, and bringing customers inside the building are all good places to start. But so too is The Executive Portfolio Wall.

The first principle of **flow**, before making any decisions from good social interaction, is to taste before you serve. Try things out.

Here once again are your main ingredients:

- The Customer Wall

- The Executive Wall

- The Culture Wall

- The Digital Business Wall

- The Executive Portfolio Wall

- The Evaluation Wall

- The Project Wall

- The Team Kanban Wall

- The Risks and Issues Wall
- Fun Walls and Job Walls
- Obeya
- The Academy or Learning Wall
- Cool Walls, Sail Boats, Blue Ocean, Friday Stories
- The Mosaic Metaphor
- The Horizons Wall
- Really Simple Metrics
- Very Subtle Gamification

You cannot cook all this at once without making a mess. So take your pick.

The whole point of **flow** is to create your own. Our Walls are there to be adapted and augmented, and you and your colleagues need to assess, trial, and adopt (or not adopt). Typically, it takes about two years to create really good **flow**. So what will be your first step?

Taking up The Customer Wall is a good way to start, because it appears unthreatening. You may hit a problem, though, for that very reason. What your Customers want may not fit with the CEO's top priorities. You have good information there but your diplomacy skills need to be well honed if you are to force customer needs further into the enterprise.

You could start with The Executive Portfolio Wall. This has special value if the company faces resource issues, since that Wall will free up money. If you are ready with some experience of the Customer Wall before tearing down the CEO's horse pictures or art collection for the Executive Portfolio Wall, that's a good place to be.

But you may also want to start with The Jobs Wall or Fun Walls, because maybe you don't quite believe what we are saying.

Maybe you don't yet have full confidence in your people. And if you do not, then they are not going to have confidence in you. That relationship is absolutely a two-way mirror.

Get everyone together for Friday Story and ask folks what they think. Chances are, this is your best possible start point, with your people guiding you to a better plan, a more realistic schedule, and a better way to lead.